THE
POET

Spring 2020

WAR & BATTLE

Published by THE POET

ISBN: 9798629604594

W: www.ThePoetMagazine.org
E: Robin@ThePoetMagazine.org

OTHER COLLECTIONS FROM THE POET

WINTER 2019 - THE SEASONS
Thirty-four poets from around the world all writing on the theme of THE SEASONS.

80 poems.
129 pages.

Paperback ISBN: 9798600084445
Kindle ASIN: B083ZKQWVJ

AUTUMN 2019 - LOVE
Teenty-nine poets from around the world all writing on the theme of LOVE.

73 poems.
119 pages.

Paperback ISBN: 9781699169612
Kindle ASIN: B07Z241YMD

CONTENTS

159. John Tunaley - ENGLAND
163. Eftichia Kapardeli - GREECE
167. Anna Banasiak - POLAND
169. LindaAnn LoSchiavo - USA
173. Mantz Yorke - ENGLAND
177. Fred Krake - USA
179. Mike Rollins - KAZAKHSTAN/ENGLAND
183. Malcolm Judd - ENGLAND
185. Donna Zephrine - USA
189. Mary Anne Zammit - MALTA
193. R. Bremner - USA
197. Brian Langley - AUSTRALIA

www.ThePoetMagazine.org

Norbert Hirschhorn
&
Fouad M. Fouad
USA and SYRIA

Dr. Fouad is a Syrian physician and well-published poet from Aleppo, now with his family in Lebanon. Norbert Hirschhorn is also a physician and poet, who until this summer lived for over a decade in Lebanon. Norbert and Dr. Fouad work together to translate each other's poetry. Several of these translations have been published in leading UK journals (*POEM, Magma*).
E: bertzpoet@yahoo.com
W: www.Bertzpoet.com

KILLERS LIVE LONG

Killers live long.
They have time to water plants in their gardens,
and once in while go to the theatre.
When necessary, they replace old dentures
with new ones fit for biting.
Elderly killers,
their bones rattle while jogging the seashore.
Ribbons of blood dribble behind them
like a crippled dog.

*

Killers mince cured meat with a kitchen knife
and lick the tang of salt left on their fingers.
'White tiles'
is how I describe their kitchens.
'Salt'
is how the killers
preserve their memories.

*

The street is potholed by knees.
Blind sounds echo off walls.
What was once an arm is now a rope.
The corpse across the road belongs to no one,
not even to One-Eye on the roof
who stitches up rag dolls,
leaving puddles of blood clotting on Nikes.

By Fouad M. Fouad co-translated from the Arabic with Norbert Hirschhorn

THE WALL ARTIST OF ALEPPO

No end. I wake to a rain of nuts + bolts
+ stink of diesel. I go to sleep by
candle light + crackling roar of a building's
collapse next door. I dream a digital dial
counting the dead, spinning faster + faster.
By day I paste manifestos on
remaining walls, scrawl poems + curses.
Nearly nothing left to eat.

I say what I want + say what I don't want.
I want to shake the world by its shoulders -
it's like touching a shade, a hologram.

I read in my holy book the myth of
resurrection, while barrels from the sky
feed real people, our mouths wide open.

By Fouad M. Fouad co-translated from the Arabic with Norbert Hirschhorn.

CANON LENS 18-300 MM

Perhaps a time to water plants growing
by a fallen wall, a shattered alley
in the black-and-white city named Aleppo.

In the gap between two houses, a sparrow
trembles in a child's hand, and a sniper
combs his pomaded hair behind a stack

of books shielding against death from the sky.
Inside the church an angel, wings outstretched,
pierced by tears and bullets, and a boy

smutched with dust, laughing. The sniper sucks
seeds from a pomegranate, lets his rifle
rest against a wall. In Aleppo.

In Aleppo, Death grows in alleys like a
rotted plant, pours from the sky:
nuts, bolts, TNT and chlorine.

Death stares into the mirror
for one moment, turns, sights,
pulls the trigger.

People on bread lines know all this.
Also children reciting in school.
And a hunchbacked old man.

By Fouad M. Fouad co-translated from the Arabic with Norbert Hirschhorn. Written as an introduction to a photo exhibit *Alep Point Zero*, by Mozaffer Salman, Paris, May 2015.

Naida Mujkic
BOSNIA & HERZEGOVINA

Naida Mujkic has published six books of poetry. She survived the Bosnian war and currently lives in Bosnia & Herzegovina.
E: naida.mujkic@yahoo.com

ELDER TREE

It was lovely at Hasiba's
Summer kitchen she used
In winter
As a matter of fact, she wasn't just cooking there
She was receiving women there
She was cutting pilaf there, she was making preserves there
It was a place for dining and sleeping
She would take us into the house and show us around
Both stories of the house
We only never went into the bedroom
With a balcony where Hasiba's son was sleeping all the time
Tough and sturdy guy
We would tiptoe back
To the summer kitchen
Where a tea pot was waiting for us
An elder tree tea
So tasty and so sweet
I would fall asleep in the corner listening to
Knitting needle clicking
Women have always had something to talk about
And they were happy with their knitting work

But one day the war – why? – took away
Hasiba's only son and soon
The green grass covered him
She got ill for short while
And died of sorrow not seeing the end of the war
Her husband locked the summer kitchen
But he too soon washed
Ashore the river half eaten up
The summer kitchen inherited
A cousin living in America, who never came over

These days the kitchen is decayed, only
Stone walls are there through which elder trees
are branching out
And those not fearing snakes are going there gladly
To collect elder tree flowers, as big as flames

Philip Meersman
BELGIUM

Brussels based Belgian multilingual poet/performer Philip Meersman pushes boundaries of poetry in both written and spoken form, drawing on current affairs, socio-political and environmental issues. His poems range from narrative and traditional form to directives for performance pieces, to concrete studies of sound, individual words and even letters themselves. He performed his work on every continent (except Antarctica), and his poetry is translated into more than 15 languages. Co-founder of several art-poetry-music-performance groups, member of the Akademia Zaum, curator of *poetryfest.brussels* and coordinating the informal Worldwide Network of Poetry Slam Championships. Meersman studied Archaeology and Art History in Brussels and he is currently doing a PhD in the Arts at the Royal Academy of Arts in Antwerp researching visual poetry, its performance strategies based upon the writings of René Magritte, Velimir Chlebnikov and the Russian Cubo-Futurists. He published *This is Belgian Chocolate: Manifestations of Poetry* (2014, NY, Three Rooms Press), and *Manifest voor de Poëzie* (Contrabas Uitgeverij).
E: philip.meersman@gmail.com
W: www.threeroomspress.com/authors/philip-meersman/
W: www.ap-arts.be/onderzoek/orale-uitvoering-van-visuele-poezie

9/11 MEMORIAL/ONE WTC

So there you are
Your existence is real
carved in stone
nor name nor body
but yet so alive
in the eyes of so many
passers-by selfie-ing themselves with you
at yet another
landmark
in yet another
city
on yet another
continent
but You, You will not see
L'Origin du Monde
no strolls along the Hudson
no cruise on the Nile
no bathing in the Ganges
no Schöne Blaue Donau
no voyage to The Heart of Darkness

Water of life
falls down
perpetual motion
bringer of life
an inundation of tears
make emotions freeze
clean-shaven cheeks
turn red

Memories of my twins -
they do not understand -
others just watch, point, picture
click-shutter-click
blink of an eye
capture the void
wait in line to see more memorial

There is a horseman behind a double fence
praising freedom and revenge
a body for an eye
click-shutter-click

the blink of an eye
all is gone
a final blow
cloud of dust

The wind strikes me
ice cold
reality cripples my bones
the Hudson flows before my eyes
joggers with apps
dogs show dog owners
encounter TV-staring strangers
another selfie
click-shutter-click
blink of an eye
all eyes on dog
woof good girl sit bye
the dog wants to move on
wants to pee
mark territory - I was here -
so other dogs
know
she was there.

Would You have liked dogs?
Playdoh, dolls or cars
Mickey or Spiderman?
Would you have wanted to become
ballet dancer or fire fighter?
Or would you have preferred to write
on a bench
on the banks of the Hudson
in the freezing cold?

As I feel the kicks of my unborn child
I tell tales to a tummy
of water
bringing life

This poem was dedicated to Dianne T. Singer and Jennifer L. Howley and their unborn children.

NO NIGHTINGALES IN NICOSIA

There we are, the not so anonymous authors taking their stance in
the circle
lavender, royalty, his-story, central eclecticisms
building relations, high society, fairy tale footprints
a room and a view
A dancing dervish taints the wall on the other side
in a no-man's-land a watchtower not watching no man no land
a perfectly circular city scarred by his-story

again

her story rubs salt on her baby
her story seems lost in translation
her story sheds salted tears
faith boxes people
calves to be led
to the altar of slaughter
to be boxed

again

nails hammer
lids close
cheaper options
in human composting
moral compasses turn
go warn the women
"be mourning mothers!"

again

he gates of hell are slowly opened
by the arms of tweeting men
in is poured the ammunition stored
out swarm the mortals in misery
screams on screens are duly documented
sorrows posted on profile pages
empathy is a distance to bridge

But there are no nightingales in Nicosia, tonight
except in the karaoke bar
we scream at screens and selfie our stream
we forget, we feast, are a one-minute star
we saw, we gave, we discuss, and we wave

we forget our fears in a mourning jar
sleepwalking in genocide

                                            again

Inspired by the visit to Platres, Nicosia (both sides of the Green Line) and the discussions amongst the poets at the 4th International Literary Festival, to the sea-girt shores of Cyprus, November 27 – December 1, 2019.

Patricia Smekal
CANADA

Patricia Smekal (a.k.a. Jazz) lives by the sea on Vancouver Island, B.C., Canada. She and her husband went to Australia on their honeymoon, in 1961. They stayed for twenty-nine years before returning to Canada. Now widowed, Pat considers Oz to be a second home, and frequently visits friends there. Pat's poetry has been winning prizes since 2003, and has appeared in over 70 print publications, in Canada and abroad. In 2009 her chapbook *Praise without Mortar* was launched. *Small Corners* was published in 2012, followed by a collaboration of poems with David Fraser called *Maybe We Could Dance*, in 2013. Yet another collaboration with Ian Cognito, titled *flora, fauna and h. sapiens*, came out in 2017. Pat frequently reads her poetry at spoken-word events on Vancouver Island and beyond.
E: jazzsmekal@shaw.ca

STONEY CREEK: JUNE 6, 1813

Today the wash runs clear.
But these old and sober stones,
unshifted by time's rush and swell,
must remember well
the war-stained waters
of that moonless night...

drowsy fields
black unwary air
muffled British bootfalls
muskets hushed
whispered password
bayonet attack
gunfire flashes
battle's cry and crack
confusion
chaos
neighing horses
troops in disarray

These old and sombre stones were there
when morning,
bright as blood,
spread its scarlet dawn across the creek,
crept through dying smoke
to light the feckless scene -
a farrago of fallen
weapons,
steeds,
and men.
Though Time's fresh melt
has cleansed the bed and lifted
lesser pebbles on their way,
these old and stolid stones remain
unscathed, unshifted
since that fifty-minute fray
which granted fame to Stoney Creek
and fixed its name
in history.

Footnote: The battle of Stoney Creek was short and bloody. Mainly due to the surprise element, the British defeated the Americans, and thus ensured that the War of 1812 was won for Upper Canada.

Mark Blickley
USA

Mark is a New York writer and proud member of the Dramatists Guild and PEN American Center. He is the author of *Sacred Misfits* (Red Hen Press), *Weathered Reports: Trump Surrogate Quotes from the Underground* (Moira Books) and the 2019 text-based art book in collaboration with artist Amy Bassin, *Dream Streams* (Clare Songbirds Publishing House). His video collaborations with Ms. Bassin, *Speaking in Bootongue* and *Widow's Peek: The Kiss of Death* will represent the United States in the year-long international world tour of *Time Is Love: Universal Feelings: Myths & Conjunctions*. The screenings kicked off last month in Madrid, organized by the esteemed African curator, Kisito Assangni.
E: blickwords@yahoo.com

A HEADS-UP DREAM FOR PEACE

I resent when beheading videos go viral and zombie apocalypses top viewer entertainment lists as it makes it much too easy for them to ignore the walking dead sharing a subway ride on way to a final destination that proves being heads up simply exposes one as too easy a target regardless of the helmet I first wear in boot camp when angry drill sergeants scream at me during squadron manoeuvrers to pull my head out of my ass so I don't kill my buddies because of a lack of concentration though I was concentrating real hard when Happy Jack took the two shots to the head that exploded his Chicago style ghetto humor all over my face and flak jacket dripping down inside sand coated combat boots that allow me to walk away and proclaim heads you lose but tales you win if you're alive and able to speak of them to a passenger audience who bury their heads in smart phone images and sounds to avoid their neighbor's headless pain of surrender seated alone across the aisle where no one else sits to coax a face from my torn and stained civilian clothes while the train chugs to the South Ferry final stop where a whiff of rusty river replaces my body odor and signals a free boat ride that promises freedom when midway to Staten Island it glides past the Statue of Liberty and I plunge towards the crowned Lady who will read my DD214 safely wrapped in protective plastic and pinned to my pants pocket along with instructing letter that will guide me towards my very own plot of land in lovely Virginia where I can sleep with silent brothers and sisters and share a peace my grateful government will mark and preserve with a uniformly crafted and informative headstone...

Excerpted from the 2019 text based art book collaboration *Dream Streams,* with fine arts photographer Amy Bassin. First published in *SUICIDE – A collection of poetry and short prose from writers around the world on the themes of suicide and self-harm.*

Lynn White
WALES

Lynn is an English woman living in north Wales. Her work is influenced by issues of social justice and events, places and people she has known or imagined. She is especially interested in exploring the boundaries of dream, fantasy and reality. She was shortlisted in the Theatre Cloud War Poetry for Today competition, and has been nominated for a Pushcart Prize and a Rhysling Award. Her poetry has appeared in many publications including: *Apogee, Firewords, Capsule Stories, Light Journal* and *So It Goes*.
E: glanypwll3@googlemail.com
W: www. lynnwhitepoetry.blogspot.com
FB: @Lynn-White-Poetry-1603675983213077

GROUND FORCE GAZA

Another volley of stones.
It's frightening.
Lucky we're protected
with our body armour.
Lucky we're safe inside our tanks.
Frightening though.
So many stones.
Such big rocks lobbed
by such little people.
We're not allowed to kill them
if they're under twelve.
And orders are orders.
But it's difficult to tell
sometimes.
Could be worse though.
Could be in a war zone
with phosphorous flying
and armour piercing shells
doing more then scratch the paint.
We could be fried alive in our tanks
then.
But now,
here,
only us can do the frying.

First published by Vagabond Press in *The Border Crossed Us - An Anthology To End Apartheid,* October 2015.

NOW AND THEN

Now the clouds are pressing down
making everything grey,
everything misty.
It's impossible to discern which way
people are facing.
It looks like everyone
is facing both ways,
so it is impossible to know who to follow,
impossible to know which path to take,
which is the good and which is bad.

Then, in the old days
it was all so clear.
This was the way.
These were the good guys,
the brave guys with the guns,
sending out their scouts
from the circled wagons
of peaceful pioneers
in search of a better life
in the vast empty land.
Protecting them from
the bad guys,
the savages,
the cowardly braves
with the bows and arrows
and scalping knives.

It didn't always go to plan.
But the cavalry usually
arrived just in time.
And the good guys
always won
in the end.

Didn't they?

First published in *Setu*, February 2017.

ONE LAST TIME

Before the trees begin to fall
I'll take a walk
through the woods
one last time,
hear the leaves glistening
and shaking
in fear of what is to come
some are already fallen
lying
dying,
it's the season for it
after all.
I'll see the light shining
lighting on the leaves of grass
that push soft spikes of green life
in between the fallen
see the light shining
through the trees
one last time.
It lights up the white crosses
chalked on the trunks
as it passes by
too many white crosses
all ready
to mark the graves
of the fallen.
It's the season for it
after all,
always the season for it
one more time.

First published in *Endlessly Rocking, Whitman Anthology*, 2019.

Aleksey Porvin
&
Isaac Stackhouse Wheeler
RUSSIA and USA

Aleksey is a Russian poet born in 1982. English translations of his poems can be found in *World Literature Today, Cyphers, Saint-Petersburg Review, Ryga Journal, SUSS, Words Without Borders, Fogged Clarity, The Straddler, The Dirty Goat, Action Yes, Barnwood International Poetry Mag, Otis Nebula, New Madrid, The Cafe Review, The New Formalist* etc. Porvin is the author of three collections of poems in Russian: *Darkness is White* (Argo-Risk Press, Moscow, 2009), *Poems* (New Literature Observer Press, Moscow 2011), and *The sun of the ship's detailed rib* (INAPRESS, Saint-Petersburg, 2013). His first book of poems translated into English, *Live By Fire*, was published by Cold Hub Press in 2011. Poems by Porvin have recently been short-listed by Andrey Bely Prize (2011, 2014). Aleksey Porvin is the winner of the Russian Debut Prize (2012).

Isaac is an American poet and literary translator best known for his renderings of novels by great contemporary Ukrainian author Serhiy Zhadan, published by Deep Vellum and Yale University Press, in collaboration with co-translator Reilly Costigan-Humes. His work has appeared in numerous journals, including *Little Star, Trafika Europe*, and the *Tupelo Quarterly.*
E: isaacswheeler@gmail.com

THREE POEMS BY ALEKSEY PORVIN
Translated from the Russian by Isaac Stackhouse Wheeler

1.

The wounds of the earth are covered by troop movements,
yet it seems healthy, so crowded with talkative forces
that there is only room for a borderlands poet
whose silence is alive thanks to the collision of states.

At night, we can't get the beeping out of our heads—
guidance systems—baby birds so accurate they've alighted
in our words. Just try talking. Half of your speech
will be muffled by hungry beaks that seek the enemy.

When you look in the sky, it's right there: the shadow of a page
or the shadow of a wing, settling on your eyes
so the sky won't recognize you as its brother, ripping the rustling
from the trees like insignia from a uniform.

Birches long to go under the axe
as strongly as they long to cross the border,
if only to be uninvolved in the collective
subject that has replaced the country's soul.

The story of how it happened is told
by the torn-out pages of newsprint chronicles
and the pixelated eyes of interviewed prisoners,
their speech muffled by beeping.

2.

On the top floor, a man washes windows,
feeling gravity, ready to grasp him
and carry him away to where shells and bullets
end up when they miss their targets.

That's the problem with firearms;
whatever you're shooting for, misses ultimately end
up in the earth, but this news does not make
the typographical ink any denser, does not fill it with rage.

That is the order of things, making holes in the earth
as if they were windows into some other, better life

but all windows get dusty, and especially these ones,
with untruth billowing up around them.

Once the windows are washed, they must be wiped
with newspapers–this old-fashion method maintains
that there is lead in typographical ink, and it helps
the windows to be more transparent, makes their shine stronger.

There is lead in typographical ink, and this newspaper
has more of it, for suddenly everything can been seen clearly;
everything has been divided into us and them,
but where is the "us?" Where are our allies?

There's clearly a whole lot of lead in this newspaper;
that means a reduction somewhere else,
where the bullets haven't reached the necessary weight,
haven't participated in applying the laws of physics.

3.

"When I was in captivity, there was only one thing that saved me. I
would close my eyes imagine my garden, that I was planting and
watering. -from an interview with a woman freed from captivity

Sit with me, brother, on the bank;
the river carries shreds of draft cards,
the ashes of burnt roads, the bitterness of blossoming,
petals from flower-windmills that bloomed early,

far too early, at the very moment
when the air thickened with flying bullets
and enveloped the smell of flowers impenetrably
as transparent polyethylene.

In plastic bags, someone wraps up
shell casings, our memories, handfuls of native soil.
There's no smelling anything through the polyethylene
or picking up a trail.

In vain, the military dogs take this white time in through their nostrils
- runaways can't be tracked down; they are clamped tight
like grains of wheat. The millstones of darkness and indifference turn,
flour pours from the sky.

It rains on hungry tongues, on speech
that lives half-starved behind barbed wire;

memories of one's native garden
walk the perimeter of the soul like sentries.

Sit with me, brother, hear about the green
cucumber shoots rising, the grape vine
gaining new flesh in the snow that has grown thick
and will soon rustle with the leaves.

The leaves have long since matured; all that remains
is to transplant them to new stalks; here is a peace agreement,
here is a release order, and here are all the draft cards, ready to
rustle, too;
they rose from the ashes, a heaven-blue seal stamped on each.

Madeline Artenberg
USA

Before falling for poetry, Madeline was a photojournalist and street theatre performer. Her poetry has appeared in many print and online publications, such as *Vernacular* and *Rattle*. *The Old In-and-Out*, a play based on her poetry and that of Karen Hildebrand, had a sold-out run in 2013. She won Lyric Recovery and Poetry Forum prizes, was semi-finalist in Margie, *The American Journal of Poetry* contest and Honourable Mention in the 2017 Highland Park Poetry Challenge. She is a regular feature on the New York City poetry circuit and has performed on Barnard Radio, Columbia Radio, Teachers and Writers Collaborative and on cable TV. For almost two decades, she has been co-producing The Alternative New Year's Day Spoken Word Extravaganza in New York City.

E: madderpoet@erols.com
E: madderpoet.MA@gmail.com

TIBET, LAND OF THE SNOWS

Bound by bamboo to mist mountain,
panda haunch-sits hungry
in the tree den:
a distraught Buddha.

Lumbers about for food,
spies two blank eyes.
Rocks shift, reveal
a monk's body.

Panda slumps safe
against shrub.
Padded feet hook
a bamboo shoot,

growing through a hole
in the monk's riddled chest.
Eating bamboo, eating bamboo -
end-to-blood-soaked-end.

Previously published, *Pudding House*, 2010.

SISTER

Imagine being that nun in Guatemala,
the one who got burnt with cigarettes
one hundred-eleven times.
Can your eyes trace the path
of a cigarette spelling in blisters
on your skin the word puta?
Do you hold your breath
or gasp it into the pain?

Your torturers turn minutes
of foreplay into days -
thrust church candles into you.
Puta en una capucha (whore in a habit),
they spit, batter you with their flesh.
You feel their organs grow to the size
of the wooden cross on which they nailed Jesus.
Is He testing you as you testify
to your love of Him?

Imagine they now hang you above
a local woman who's been bound -
the one who helped you
in church reading-class.
They force into your fists a machete,
press their hands down on yours to slice
the weapon across the woman's chest -
you've cut off her breasts.
You are shaking, the cut is ragged.

Or would you rather imagine being
one of the rapists?
Or their director?
Or the other woman?
Or Jesus?
Or His Father?
Choose.

Previously published, *Absinthe Literary Review*, 2005.

Linda Imbler
USA

Linda is the author of three poetry collections published by Amazon. Soma Publishing has published three of her poetry books; *The Sea's Secret Song, Pairings (*a hybrid of short fiction and poetry), and *That Fifth Element*. Since writing her first poem five years ago, her poetry and short stories have appeared both locally and internationally. In addition to putting pen and paper to inventive use, Linda is an avid reader and budding illustrator. This writer, yoga practitioner, and classical guitar player lives in Wichita, Kansas with her husband, Mike the Luthier, several quite intelligent saltwater fish, and an ever-growing family of gorgeous guitars. She has been nominated for a Pushcart Prize and several Best of the Nets.
E: mike-imbler@cox.net
Blog: lindaspoetryblog.blogspot.com

FINAL COUNT

The final count,
after the conflict,
of those left standing.
A sum of hollow, empty vessels,
not feeling the aftermath,
for the souls of the dead
carried the souls of the survivors
away with them when they took flight.

The final count
of those left standing,
looking beyond the carnage,
no longer able to imagine
what man once built
in that place where he dwelt,
constructed by desire and philosophy.

The final count
of those left standing,
the absolute scorecard designed
to identify the victors,
when all bloodshed and hostility cease.
Those left standing,
declared the heirs to triumph,
and to them is bequeathed desolation.

HAVE YOU HEARD THE BUTTERFLIES SING?

Have you heard the butterflies sing?
Rolling the quiet skies with beating wings,
Dropping men with olive green helmets from the sky,
Rocket's red glare not ceasing.

Have you heard the butterflies cry?
Like the roar of lions and panthers
At pride's decline,
Watching those same men on the ground as they die.

Have you heard the butterflies grieve?
Guttural, pleading rotors,
Leaving troops cemented to the ground,
There's nothing left for them to retrieve.

Have you heard the butterflies fall?
Silenced by jungle fire
Against the clipping of wings,
Metallic wreckage in awkward sprawl.

Butterflies scream the same as men,
Caught in a circle of human torment.
When will we learn to circumvent
So much human blood being spent?

Moinak Dutta
INDIA

Presently engaged as a teacher of English in a government sponsored institution, Moinak has been writing poems and stories from his school days. Many of his poems and stories are published in national and international anthologies and magazines, and also dailies including *Madras Courier, The Statesman* (Kolkata edition), *World Peace Poetry anthology* (United Nations), *Spillwords* (New York, USA), *Setu* (Pittsburgh, USA), *Riding and Writing* (Ohio, USA, as a featured poet twice), *The Indian Periodical, Pangolin Review, Tuck Magazine, Duane's Poetree, Story mirror, Tell me your story, Nature Writing (UK), Oddball magazine, Soft Cartel, Diff Truths' magazine, Mason Street* (literary journal of Newark Public Library, NY, USA), *Narrow Road, Ethos Literary Journal, The Literary Fairy Tales, Defiant Dreams* (a collection of stories on women empowerment), *Dynami Zois* (an anthology from authors from India and abroad), *Muffled Moans* (a special anthology against women and child abuse, gender violence) and *Quesadilla and other adventures.* Moinak has also written essays and articles on education and literature and other topics which have been published worldwide. His first full length English fiction *Online@Offline* was published in 2014. His second fiction titled *In search of la radice* was published in 2017. Moinak also worked as an editor of a poetry collection titled *Whispering Poeisis*.
E: moinakdutta@yahoo.co.in
W: www.moinakdutta.wordspress.com

SOMEWHERE TUCKED AWAY

About a decade and half
   must have passed through in between
when one day the man
   arrived at his town one wintry evening,
the bus stop where
   he got down with his sack was not the same,
for he found there
   no more that homegrown feel of a small town
the rows of deodars
   were not there too and the road seemed full
of people not known
   'where had that house gone to?' he thought
from the porch of which
   there hung coils of ivy in poesy wrought,
thinking all these
   the man walked the road till he stopped
in front of a little
   cosy looking bustling coffeeshop,
at the counter
   there was a man he thought did he know
for he had that cut
   on his forehead just over his left brow,
'You have grown old'
   was the first thing that he said to the man
who looked up
   with curious eyes and disbelief in his mind,
'you? our own Ayush?'
   the man lunged forward to him greet,
his hands he held
   and their eyes glistened quiet as they did meet,
'after so many years,
   how come here mate?' the man in tears
   uttered with joy asked him straight,
'well, I had received
   a letter from someone here unexpected,'
saying this he
   out from his coat's pocket did bring
a piece of a paper
   almost blank barring a few words written
in a known too known hand,
   'I know you have gone away to a faraway land
but please for the sake

of all the follies and the mistakes,
come at least once,
now that the war had ended and peace
had been declared
all through the country now that there are
no more sounds of sirens
and alarms of wildly ringing bells,
now that all the fire
had been doused and buried for at least
quite a few months,
come to my humble house if there is any chance;'

'Oh! you silly man! how you've come
covering thousand acres green
and a few deserts of sands,'
said the man with a trembling voice,
'Mate,you've come right, but you've lost that choice
that girl who cared to write such a thing
which she never dared
to say to you in person
had been to the another
land by the dictates sent,
the land where you could
never possibly go
for there lives she with her friends and a hoe,
there she has settled
with her garden to bloom and grow,'

Ayush heard it all
keeping quiet and low

and he thought he missed nothing
other than those deodars and rows
of trees that lined the way
and that girl who had somewhere
kept a story tucked away.

Pamela Scott
SCOTLAND

Pamela lives in Glasgow, UK. Her work has appeared in various magazines including *The Poet, Buckshot Magazine, Brilliant Flash Fiction, A Quiet Courage, Allegro Poetry Magazine* and *Dream Catcher*. She has also featured in anthologies published by Collections of Poetry and Prose and Indigo Dreams Press. She is working on her first novel and a collection of micro poetry and micro fiction focusing on love, loss and grief.

E: scootiepm26@hotmail.co.uk
FB: @pcottwriter
Twitter: @pscottwriter

STARK

nothing can prepare you
for the noise of it,
the gunfire, the endless
booms, that vibrate your
eardrums, block out sound,
the explosions everywhere

nothing can prepare you
for the horror of it,
the blood, so much of it,
the bodies, fields of dead,
the screams, flesh torn apart

they sent me home when
a bomb took out a young lad
beside me, barely eighteen,
he was shredded, felt his
blood on my face, the blast
tore my ear off

PTSD the doctor called it,
shell shocked from all I'd
seen & heard, needed rest,
space to put my broken
pieces back together

the half-deaf, broken man
they sent home, wasn't really me,
a ghost, a shell doppelgänger

anger finds me that I never had before

can only hear half of what people
say, rage flares up, shout at
everyone in my life, they suffocate
me, make me feel abandoned,
need space, want to be crushed
by their love

cannot bear the slightest noise,
even a loud voice gives me headaches

turn into an ogre

PTSD they call it, pat your
head, send you home, tell
you just to take your time,
breathe a little

they don't tell you it will
wake you in the middle of
the night, coated with sweat,
hearing the screams of the dead

they don't tell you it
will make you shake with
fear, wet yourself in the dark

Mark Andrew Heathcote
ENGLAND

Mark is from Manchester. He is the author of *In Perpetuity* and *Back on Earth*, two books of poems published by a CTU publishing group ~ Creative Talents Unleashed. Mark is adult learning difficulties support worker, who began writing poetry at an early age at school. He enjoys spending his leisure time reading and writing, and spending time gardening and enjoying the natural world.
E: mrkheathcote@yahoo.co.uk

WAR, WAR, WAR

Run, run, run children take flight
Row, row, row with all you're might
Swim, swim, swim don't-die-young
Try & try to remain upbeat & strong.

War, war, war soldier what's it all for.
Did your mother give birth to murder?
Father, Father, forgive them all we implore
Sister, sister, why do your children shudder?

War, war, war tanks & military trucks roll, roll, and roll on...
War, war, war, enemy planes by the score
Want to crush the orphanage, kill nothing more
War, war, war soldier what's all this killing for

Bastions of the faith what are you clinging on to
Your beliefs are in mortal ruins
The innocent are dying in firing squad executions
With them, you might as well be the aliens who hew & slew
Hew & slew, hew & slew, hew & slew, WAR!

IN THE DEAD OF NIGHT

I'm an oak with rings ingrain
My heart is a woodcut carving
My soul a gnarled wooden cane
No longer prevents my falling.

I'm a mountain-pine-forest
A field of flattened wheat:
A no-man's-land, a gauntlet
Thrown, down in beseech

Of-war, of-madness or friendship
Take your pick; I am ready, for all.
I have sharpened and whetted,
Sheaved my blade; heeding its call.

I have vanquished-my-enemies
One and all to see them lonesome fall
I have rewritten they're own parodies.
In my turn stood, equally tall.

I have ignited into blossom,
And unfurled to catch sight
Every flower my breath can bosom
Hold to itself in the dead of night.

K. Miller
USA

K. Miller has a PhD in English Studies, is an American living in the Midwest. She wrote this poem based off of conversations with a grandfather who served in the Korean War, also known as The Forgotten War.
E: kemiller500@gmail.com
Twitter: @MasticatedMuse

FORGOTTEN REMEMBERED

The ever-present stench of
      rotting flesh,
      acrid smoke,
      scorched earth,
      morbid decay,
seeping through heavy cotton polyester blends,
stealing oxygen and
choking ruination.

The smells are what he remembers,
the stink firmly embedded
in body and mind,
and whatever spirit
remains.
His every move trailed by
a noxious bouquet,
every night laid to rest in
an odious hellscape.
He smells it all the damn time
and can never
get away,
take cover,
and hide.

The sharp citrus of a juicy tangerine:
      seeping necrosis, exposed guts.
Freshly mown grass, damp and dewy:
      dehydrated piss, stale vomit.
Sweet jasmine perfume, a hint of lingonberry:
      burnt carbon, pungent sulfur.
Smooth whiskey, oaken malt:
      flooded excrement, foul waste.

War is an aromatic cocktail
full of sour notes and
acidic aftertastes
that refuse to be washed away
or replaced.
Olfactory triggers
      immersive episodes:
dying comrades,
the remnants of young men turned old,

brittle lips gasping his name,
stained fingers tugging his sleeves,
desperate eyes resisting closure,
corrosive lungs exhaling cigarette smoke
and ruptured lies
one last time.

Kushal Poddar
INDIA

Kushal has edited the online magazine *Words Surfacing*, and authored *The Circus Came To My Island* (Spare Change Press, Ohio), *A Place For Your Ghost Animals* (Ripple Effect Publishing, Colorado Springs), *Understanding The Neighbourhood* (BRP, Australia), *Scratches Within* (Barbara Maat, Florida), *Kleptomaniac's Book of Unoriginal Poems* (BRP, Australia) and *Eternity Restoration Project-Selected and New Poems* (Hawakal Publishers, India) and now *Herding My Thoughts To The Slaughterhouse - A Prequel* (Alien Buddha Press).
E: kpoddar2010@gmail.com

INFUSION AND IRON

Late morning. The hangover
possesses half of my head.
The other half listens to the news.

You brew some tea, albeit
by the time I sip its insipidity
it has levelled down to the room temp.

I step out to join the pogrom,
cancel two men.
When I return the gun was still hot.

THE ENDING LINE

The haze line burns from the south to the north.
Cross it and you will meet all the dodos
both demised and alive
the way we exist nowadays - within and beyond the world's end.

If you cross the line from the other end
reminiscence seems fluid, a neonatal view - chiming,
charming and caterwauling too, and so we blink,
so we stir in our after-death -
we had so much, hence so much we had blazed!

Desire, if you desire, to cross back the line, you see,
wanes the line, reclines the core existence
like one's grandfather sleeps into necrosis,
and his chair still sways.

Kashif Ilyas
INDIA

Kashif Ilyas is currently a research scholar in the Department of English, Aligarh Muslim University, India. He is an Indian, but he was born in Jeddah, Saudi Arabia, where he lived for the first eighteen years of his life. His research interests include Cultural Studies, Postmodernism and Literary Nonsense. His poetry has previously been published on the *Dead Beats Literary Blog.*
E: k.ilyas92@gmail.com
FB: @kashif.ilyas.754
Instagram: @ilyaskashif

DINNER CONVERSATIONS

The siren bleats through the night
As warplanes fly over our homes
We turn off the lights and cower under the dining table
As if memories of dinner conversations
From a time when death didn't hang over our heads
Will protect us.

The planes fly away
We lose the world's most dangerous lottery
And live to see another day.

Gordon Simmonds
ENGLAND

Born and raised in Essex, England. Gordon left school aged fifteen and joined the British Army where he discovered early on that he was a good scholar but a bad soldier. He left the Army nine years later and became what he now calls an industrial mercenary – in fact he's never had a proper job since, and has worked in, and travelled the Middle East as well as his adopted Lincolnshire. He would describe himself as a shy extrovert. If you see him on the street he's likely to be wearing a cowboy hat and boots, or a Scottish kilt and playing the bagpipes. He loves to race – either bikes or karts and once had some talent as a fencer where his hard, aggressive style achieved some notable victories. As a writer and poet his work is severely limited by work and inclination. His first poem was broadcast on the BBC while he was still at school. His next poem wasn't published until thirty-four years later.
E: gj.simmonds@outlook.com

A SOLDIER'S PRAYER

If I am to die, let it be in the heat of battle
Facing the foe with righteous anger.
Let it be quick, that the fleeting pain
Of torn flesh and broken bone tarries not.
Or, as an old man in a soft bed
Gently drifting into the great beyond.
Let it be clean, that my soul can break the bond
Of earthly endurance, and in my prideful way
Render my corpse less pitiable.

Let not the bomb or the bullet shatter my fragile limbs
That I might live a crippled life in a crippled body.
To suffer the silent stares of strangers,
The condescending concern of carers
And the helpless pity of loved ones
For as an old friend once said,
"I know there are worse things than dying."

A tribute to Eric Bogle, whose music inspires me still.

Hussein Habasch
KURDISTAN/GERMANY

Hussein is a poet from Kurdistan. He currently lives in Bonn, Germany. He writes in Kurdish and Arabic, and his poems have been translated into English, German, Spanish, French, Chinese, Turkish, Persian, Albanian, Uzbek, Russian, Italian, Bulgarian, Lithuanian, Hungarian, Macedonian, Serbian and Romanian, and has had his poetry published in a large number of international anthologies. His books include: *Drowning in Roses, Fugitives across Evros River, Higher than Desire and more Delicious than the Gazelle's Flank, Delusions to Salim Barakat, A Flying Angel, No pasarán* (in Spanish), *Copaci Cu Chef* (in Romanian), *Dos Árboles* and *Tiempos de Guerra* (in Spanish), *Fever of Quince* (in Kurdish), *Peace for Afrin, peace for Kurdistan* (in English and Spanish) and *The Red Snow* (in Chinese), He participated in many international festivals of poetry including: Colombia, Nicaragua, France, Puerto Rico, Mexico, Germany, Romania, Lithuania, Morocco, Ecuador, El Salvador, Kosovo, Macedonia, Costa Rica, Slovenia, China, Taiwan and New York City.
E: habasch70@hotmail.com

THE CHILD WHO LOST EVERYTHING

Where is my foot, I want to run after the birds?
Where is my hand, I want to clap for the butterflies?
Where is my brother, I want to play with him?
Where is my sister, I want to banter with her?
Where is my father, I want to accompany him to the market?
Where is my mother, I want to sit in her warm lap?
Where is my friends, I want to go to school with them?
The distracted child
Lost in the planes bombardment
His brother, sister, father, mother, and half of his body
Now he is lying in the field hospital
Running in his dream after the birds
Clapping for the butterflies
Playing with his brother
Bantering his sister
Accompanying his father to the market
Sitting in his mother's lap
And going to school with his friends!

SURVIVING MIRACULOUSLY

I was too small
I didn't understand what is going on around me.
My only concern in life was the milk bottle
And an affectionate touch from my mother's hand.
The adult were talking with worry
About planes and bombardments
I didn't understand what they meant
But I flinch from time to time
From its strange sound.

Today they bombed our home
I found myself between the rubble
My face and body were covered in dust.
I was so frightened
I cried, screamed, and called for help
Until they lift me up, and I miraculously survived
My mother kissed my left cheek
My father kissed the right
I felt fine
But I was so tired
I dozed off on my father forearm.
Immediately I had a dream of the milk bottle
And of that affectionate touch from my mother's hand.

THE TALE ABOUT THE GIRL WHO WENT TO THE STORE

I missed my school so much
I told my mother I will go to the nearby store
To buy a pencil, notebook, and an eraser
At the street, I was happy mumbling a song.
Suddenly I saw my blood's drops
Pouring on the ground
I felt my head
I found a bullet settled in it!
I remembered the sniper's face
Who was on the top of the building
Laughing his yellow laugh at my face.
My mother regretted letting me go alone,
She cried so much
My father cried
My brother cried
My doll cried
I was stretching my hand from heaven,
Wiping tears from their swollen eyes
And comforting their sorrowful hearts!

Megha Sood
USA

Megha is an Indian American living in Jersey City, New Jersey, USA. She is a contributing editor at *Free Verse Revolution, Heretics, Lovers and Madmen, Sudden Denouement, Whisper and the Roar, GoDogGoCafe*, and poetry editor at *Ariel Chart*. She had had published over 350 works in journals including *Better than Starbucks, FIVE:2: ONE, KOAN, Kissing Dynamite, Foliate Oak. Visitant Lit, Quail Bell, Dime show review*, etc. and has works featured in 35 upcoming anthologies in the US, UK, Australia and Canada. She is two-time State-level winner of the NJ Poetry Contest (2018/2019), National level poetry finalist in Poetry Matters Prize 2019, and shortlisted in the Pangolin Poetry Prize 2019. Works selected numerous times by Jersey City Writers group and Department of Cultural Affairs for the Arts House Festival.
E: megharani1409@gmail.com
W: meghasworldsite.wordpress.com
Twitter: @meghasood16

SYRIA - LIVING IN A WAR ZONE

Where have all the flowers
gone to die?
Why the sun never rises
and death and misery
have become part of life?

Small hands clasp the dead bits
the lanes and the gully
are marked by the cadavers
death has been
piling constantly

Screams are
gut-wrenching and numbing
the soul is burdened
by carrying the weight of
death and is slowly crumbling.

He stands alone
cold and dry,
tears streaming
from his haggard face
and he has a question
everyone should face

Why the street
he ran with his heart's content,
to fly his beautiful kite
or dusty place he hid underneath
to play the game of seeking and hide,
are all muddied
with blood and disgrace?

Where are giggles and laughs hiding?
once a place he called his home
stands a charred broken place
Barely alive.

Why are the hopes and dreams
are crouched and suffocated
in the deep thick smoke?
Where did they hide

all the broken toys
he once adored?

He stands there
confused and broken-hearted
in a country where the
love and humanity
has parted ways
and left him to rot
alone in their place.

Why the land once brimming with
luxury and grace
is defeated and defaced?

Why did all the places
he could run and play
are pitted with the makeshift
mass graves?

MISSED BOAT

My home burnt down to ashes
walls painted with new shades of gore
a new shade of limestone and grey:
with fingers dipped in the blood
of my beautiful loved souls

My streets are laced
with death and macabre
the wailing cries of widows,
his lost son - with his broken bike
eating dust evermore

With dried-up trails on the face
eyes gazing from emptiness to nothing,
has painted a picture
of a new broken being

I'm digging hopelessly
with my bloody knuckles
looking for lost hope
in the pile of death and fear
trying to cover my back
with the last piece of
borrowed bread and tattered cloth

I'm trying to keep myself alive knowing
all the faces I have known
ate and grew up with,
have been fed to the bloodhounds
in all its glory

I couldn't care less about
the orphaned kid next door
whose birth I celebrated
and danced till my feet went sore

All I care about now,
that I should run and hide
like a hunted prey
make sure not to miss the boat
which will take me
to the promised lands, far far away.

John Notley
THAILAND

John is a retired travel agent who now spends much of his time in Thailand where he attempts to write poetry and short stories. He has had moderate success in the past but still has to hit the jackpot. He regrets to note that very little rhyming poetry is published these days which, in his opinion, means that hardly any modern poetry will be remembered in years to come.

E: john.notley@gmail.com

ELEVEN ELEVEN NINETEEN-EIGHTEEN

That morning the deafening thunder of the guns ceased
silence whispered its deathly hush
and war was waged no more and all was peace.
The birds began to sing their joyful songs again
over the stilled, shelled-drilled, water-filled trenches
and noise and smoke and death gave birth to a better reign.
The war to end all wars paid in blood by thousands dead
and as they laid them in their countless graves
"We will remember them" they said.
But memories are short and soon guns spat again:
Alamein, Korea, Cambodia, Vietnam, Afghanistan
and still men spit and snarl and kill and maim.
The toll goes on and will it never end
this sickness of the mind and soul.
Are we forever to this bloody treadmill condemned?
Yet still the bugle sounds o'er Flanders' Menin Gate
and still the blood red poppies bloom
as we recall the men who died and those at home who wait.

Joan McNerney
USA

Joan's poetry has been included in many literary magazines such as *Seven Circle Press, Dinner with the Muse, Poet Warriors, Blueline, and Halcyon Days. Four Bright Hills Press Anthologies*, several *Poppy Road Review Journals*, and numerous Spectrum Publications have accepted her work. She has four Best of the Net nomination, and her latest title *The Muse In Miniature*, is now available.
E: poetryjoan@statetel.com

THE BLUE GOD

The blue god of war
is so strong
he can twist trees
with the tip of his tongue.

You better not defy him
scream at him
lie to him.
He'll explode and beat
the hell out of you.

He lives on nothing
will die for nothing
makes us children
shivering all night
crying in empty winds
turning our tears to ice.

The blue god of war
is so strong
northern winds bow to his will.

He doesn't dig
your moaning
and groaning.
You better shut up or he'll
make mincemeat out of you.

He laughs at everything
has respect for nothing
makes us afraid to fight
when he spits in our faces
turning our tears to ice.

So we watch in silence
waiting for the coming light
when he will hold us
in his burning hands
and we will be born twice
once by fire
once by ice.

Matteo Marangoni
ITALY

Matteo was born in Macerata, Italy. He is a tourist operator and the author and writer of poems and tales, and has successfully participated in a number of poetry contests and public readings. He was a founding member of several Cultural Associations, and has worked at various non-profit organizations in the field of contemporary art, tourism, culture, literature and theatre.

E: matteomarangoni74@gmail.com
FB: @matteo.marangoni.397
FB: @centroletturaarturopiatti
Twitter: @MatteoMarangoni

SPIN THE WHEEL

Downhill
in the field
limits and
borders
wars and
battles
common fronts,
illiberty and
speculation
is the Arab spring
today as then.

Justin Fox
SOUTH AFRICA

Justin is a writer and photographer based in Cape Town, South Africa. He's a former editor of *Getaway International* travel magazine. Justin was a Rhodes Scholar and received a doctorate in English from Oxford University, after which he became a research fellow at the University of Cape Town, where he now teaches part-time. His articles and photographs have appeared internationally in a number of publications and on a wide range of topics, while his short stories and poems have appeared in various anthologies. His recent books include *The Marginal Safari* (Umuzi, 2010), *Whoever Fears the Sea* (Umuzi, 2014) and *The Impossible Five* (Tafelberg, 2015). Justin has also contributed to *THE SEASONS, TRAVEL, LOVE* and *WAR* in the Collections of Poetry and Prose series.
E: justinfoxafrica@gmail.com

WAR ON THE TELLY

A Hutu hand quivers for food
beneath a barred Kigali door
in a prison land of the insane
where brother eats of brother:
the eye knows no weeping for this,
aid workers stand with open hands,
children in the face of it.

Waves of blue and green
and swathes of yellow
ignite this Coliseum of light:
it's Brazil versus Sweden
in the Bowl of Roses
where tribal colours delight.

The news is done,
the victors won,
he extinguishes the blue flame
and surrenders to sleep.

Somewhere in the night
he wakes, afraid.
There's scratching at the door.
Slow, persistent.
Is it a rat, perhaps a hand?
If a rat, will it run riot
when he opens?
If a hand…

He sprays poison beneath the door,
burns paper through the crack
to terrify and put to flight.
To no avail,
it claws on.
He stops the gap with newspaper
and awaits the cavalry of dawn.

Mid-morning he awakes,
dons spectacles and gown,
and, light-emboldened,
with cricket bat in hand,
he stalks the door.

With his heart he twists the handle
and, club raised, draws quickly open.
At his feet a young dove lies,
ever asleep in a bed of
burnt paper feathers.

Raji Unnikrishnan
INDIA/BAHRAIN

"A woman so passionately in love with words, a mother and a journalist. Indian, based in Bahrain, I work with the *Gulf Daily News*. Life has taught me much over time, and my writings are raw reflections of what I have seen and experienced. Poetry gives me the wings to fly into that sublime world of joy and peace. I cry, smile and laugh while I write or read poetry, which for me is the best genre of literature. It frees my thoughts to soar high and it helps me swim deep into the depth of my dreams. I use my pen name 'desert rose' abbreviated as ~dr, reflecting the fragrance of those blooms which show up once a year on the outskirts of the arid land.
E: rajiunnikrishnan@gmail.com
FB: @RajiUnnikrishnan
Instagram: @raji111
Instagram:@a_de_sert_rose
Facebook Blog – Desert Rose
Twitter: @rajiukrishnan
LinkedIn: @RajiUnnikrishnan

REFUGEE

My home,
I turned around,
to look at the abode of joy,
my heart thumped heavily.

It is war,
and I have to flee. I glanced,
one last time – my home,
holding my tot to my bosom.

My thatch behind,
Laugher echoed from within,
of a family simple, but joyful;
with less, but enough.

Sunny were the days,
farms green and lush;
lovely were the nights
lanterns lit the verandah.

Oh, I forgot the painted pot
precious it was, a gift.
Life is prized; I fled, while a piece
of my heart opted to stay back.

Once more, I turned -
the smoky scene broke me.
My home, no more. Instead,
lay a heap of shattered dreams.

Clasping my life on to me,
and scraps of nothings,
I tried to run, to a boat,
my feet and heart heavy.

The skiff swayed,
my heart quivered.
I held him closer to myself
to my bosom, all the more.

Waters deep, waves high,
one splash and I regret!

Man's selfish reflex and
I lost my bundle of joy!

He slipped through my fingers!
Beating my sorry chest
I wailed loud, but
the roaring surf killed it.

Washed ashore, lay
a tiny frame, like a doll.
My priceless possession -
cold and numb, without a smile.

I tried to warm him
with all the flames of a dream
and memories that filled my chest,
but he lay frozen.

I am a refugee.
Barefoot, in rags, I wait
behind barbed fence.
I am a number, not anymore a name.

Wasn't war better?
I wished I was crushed
with my dreams right there -
my home, sweet home.

Dedicated to all those who are forced to flee and the three-year-old Alan Kurdi, the Syrian boy of
Kurdish ethnic background whose image made global headlines after he drowned in the Mediterranean
Sea, as part of the Syrian refugee crisis, on Sept 2, 2015.

Bruce Louis Dodson
SWEDEN

Bruce Louis Dodson is an expat living in Borlänge, Sweden, where he writes fiction and poetry. His most recent work has appeared in: *Foreign & Far Away – Writers Abroad Anthology, Sleeping Cat Books – Trip of a Lifetime Anthology, Northern Liberties Review, Pirene's Fountain, Tic Toc and Storm Cycle Anthologies - Kind of a Hurricane Press, Vine Leaves, Cordite Poetry Review, Buffalo Almanac, mgversion2>datura, Maintenant 11, Glassworks, Door Is A Jar, Popshot, Proverse Poetry Prize Anthology, So It, Goes, Blood and Bourbon, Ancient Paths, Whispers To Roars, Pure Slush, and Without Words Anthology.*
E: 2crows@earthlink.net

TOO LATE SMART

Old Men
Know youth
Far better than the young
Regret the loss of strength
And daring fearless
Knowing what might possibly befall
Beyond recall
Loss of naivety
Unmissed
War's gun smoke and excitement
Are replaced
With sense of needless loss
In places far from home
Much glorified in printed words exultant
More than these.

First published: *Tic Toc Anthology* - Kind of a Hurricane Press, 2014.

BUSHIDO STEEL

Only the winter wind surrounds me.
Soldiers do not come to look for death
Inside this cave
My sword's calligraphy is perfect.
Brush of steel
Red ink on white snow.

First published: *Pirene's Fountain*, 2014.

Eliza Segiet
POLAND

Eliza graduated with a Master's Degree in Philosophy, completed postgraduate studies in Cultural Knowledge, Philosophy, Arts and Literature at Jagiellonian University. Her poems *Questions* and *Sea of Mists* won the title of the International Publication of the Year 2017 and 2018 with Spillwords Press. Her poem *The Sea of Mists* was chosen as one of the best amidst the hundred best poems of 2018 by International Poetry Press Publication, Canada. In The 2019 Poet's Yearbook, as the author of *Sea of Mists,* she was awarded with the prestigious Elite Writer's Status Award as one of the best poets of 2019. Her poem *Order* was selected as one of the 100 best poems of 2019 in International Poetry Press Publications, Canada. Nominated for the Pushcart Prize 2019, nominee for Naji Naaman Literary Prize 2020, nominated for the iWoman Global Awards 2020. Eliza's works can be found in anthologies and literary magazines worldwide.
E: eliza.anna@op.pl

EVIL ONES
Translated by Artur Komoter

Will we be able to tell
that there were those
who killed the future?

In the roar of the shots,
we try to whisper life.

The eyes speak only with silence:
- *we are afraid of death.*

Life is
- trembling.
Despite all this
it is hope for another
- smile of chance.

Perhaps because of it
the evil ones
will not hear our silence?

OTHER
Translated by Artur Komoter

On the cadaverous hand
the inarticulate armbands
with the Star of David said:

here goes the Other,

The pronounced one in the crowd
whispered:

those who protect me -
let me keep
my dignity

but he wondered
whether life
is good -
not worse than death?

SIDE OF LIFE AND DEATH
Translated by Artur Komoter

People on the right,
Jews on the left.
Her sister was caught into the wagon,
they wanted her too.

She fled between
the Gestapo's widely spaced legs.
She ran home.

- Dad, daddy,
they hid Krysia on the train.
Take her.

He redeemed his daughter.

It's nothing that now
it won't be enough for bread.

Rozalia Aleksandrova
BULGARIA

Rozalia Aleksandrova lives in Plovdiv, Bulgaria. Author of 11 poetry books: *The House of My Soul* (2000), *Shining Body* (2003), *The Mystery of the Road* (2005), *The Eyes of the Wind* (2007), *Parable of the key* (2008), *The Conversation between Pigeons* (2010), *Sacral* (2013), *The Real Life of Feelings* (2015), *Pomegranate from Narrow* (2016), *Brushy* (2017), *Everything I did not say* (2019). Editor and compiler of over ten literary almanacs, collections and anthologies. She is a member of the Union of Bulgarian Writers. In March 2006 she created a poetic-intellectual association Quantum and Friends for the promotion of quantum poetry in civil society, Plovdiv and Bulgarian phenomenon. Initiator and organizer of the International Festival of Poetry SPIRITUALITY WITHOUT BORDERS from 2015.
E: rozalia54@yahoo.com
FB: @Розалия Александрова

ANSWER TO DEATH

You ask me about the war?
When the whole Earth craves peace.
When mothers cover the sands
with baby bodies. And a dream.

You ask me about the war.
I don't come from there.
I wasn't there when
the laughter of evil broke out.
When the moon was gathering hearts.

You ask me about the war.
The one that has never been in me.
Neither in you, nor in the woman,
mourning men and brothers.
Weeping bitterly over the son's tomb.

You don't ask me for strength,
by which God tests children.
That power came out
from the shell of the visible,
across the Dead Sea,
froze in hopes of dunes.

You ask me about the past.
I live now.
I live in the future.
Indestructible by the illusions of fear.
Invincible for dark plans.

Ask me about the light.

Mark Fleisher
USA

Mark served in the U.S. Air Force from April 1965 to September 1968, including a year in Vietnam as a combat news reporter assigned to Headquarters 7th Air Force Directorate of Information (DXI). He received a Bronze Star for Meritorious Service among other decorations. Now a resident of Albuquerque, New Mexico, the Ohio University journalism graduate has published three books of poems, many dealing with his Vietnam experiences. His work has appeared in numerous online and print anthologies.
E: markfleisher111@gmail.com

BUNKER MENTALITY

A helluva way to die,
wondering if I'd see
my next birthday,
huddled like a rat
in the damp dank darkness
of a bunker reinforced
with sandbags and steel plates,
hearing the mortar shells
overhead, praying short rounds
do not test our protection
Yes praying, because there are
no atheists in foxholes or
in bunkers for that matter

So much for the New Year's truce

Bullets whizzing about,
ricocheting off the walkway
leading from my hootch
to the latrine sent me
scrambling to the bunker
Praise the Lord and pass
the ammunition, only there
is no ammo, no weapons,
we are non-combatants
or so we are told; tell that
to Victor Charlie with
the AK-47 and his pal with
the RPG launcher

So much for the New Year's truce

An eternity passes before
the welcome staccato chatter
of machine guns rakes
the tall grass bordering
our living quarters; then
the whoosh of rockets
destroying the mortar tubes,
Cobras spitting their venom,
assuring these invaders
will not live to fight another day

Tet January 1968
From Tan Son Nhut Air Base
Happy New Year to all.

CAN THO

Vietnamese restaurant near
The Cleveland Park Metro
Washington, D.C.
Autumn 1986

Sipping corn and crab soup
inhaling perfume of flavours
talking with the owner,
he came from
Can Tho
in the Mekong Delta

Can Tho, spring of 1968

my photographer Sam and I
in the makeshift operating room
in the ramshackle hospital,
awed by Air Force force surgeons
pulling away the mangled flesh
and shattered bone -
all that's left -
one side of the woman's face,
collateral damage,
the cynical gift from chunks of metal
delivered by one army or another
only she knows - maybe

the docs give her a new jaw,
a reconstructed cheekbone,
in time she will eat solid food,
talk to her children,
sing to her grandchildren,
and I know she will thank the docs,
and I know she will curse,
one army... or another... or both.

INTO THE DARKENED FRAY
(A Civil War Poem)

Gentlemen of high-born birth
sought not their faces bloodied
so gladly paid without remorse
to keep their boots unmuddied

With bounty dollars in pockets full
from meadows of Cork and Kerry
with rifles resting on shoulders blue
from green fields of Clare and Derry

Cries of the wounded in thickened brogues
heard above the volleys of musket fire
one-by-one, two-by-two they fell
upon the battlefield's burning pyre

Sabers glared in the sun's dense haze
riders charged on cavalry mount
cut down by artillery barrage
dying breaths not even God can count

The raw recruit not yet a score
saved the colours when the bearer fell
he carried with pride the Union flag
into the fire and smoke of hell

Surgeons' tattered tent bathed in red
arms and legs sawn asunder
striving to save a soldier's being
as cannonballs roared athunder

The silent slain sheltered by blankets coarse
awaiting departure from the field
returned in grief to mothers old
whose shattered hearts are never healed

The preacher read words from the holy book
speaking to a power high above
O,, with six hundred thousand souls to die
how to talk of brotherly love

Mourners wept and said their prayers

on roughened knees to kneel
church bells echoed across the countryside
sounding a sullen and sombre peal

Alas, they laid the lad to rest
beside a loved one's grave
for sadly his beribboned father
also slept amongst the brave

Generations fly like symbolic birds
yet some hold to the unjust cause
let one nation's people come together
overcoming ancient faults and ancient flaws

Kev Milsom
ENGLAND

Kev originates from the historic English port of Bristol, although he now resides in the semi-rural area of Stonehouse, in Gloucestershire. He is approaching the latter stages of his 5th decade far too quickly for his liking, but is uncertain what to do about this in practical terms. When he is not writing down the never-dull oddness that permeates his mind and attempting to weave it into creative writing, he can be found in the worlds of genealogy, music and parapsychology. His beard changes colour regularly, because that's simply how things are meant to be. Currently, it is bright green to reflect the approaching day of St. Patrick and to celebrate the large ratio of Irish blood swilling around his veins. He is quite certain that St. Patrick would approve of his beard hue and this makes him very happy.
E: kevmilsom@yahoo.co.uk

TO FOLLOW IN FAEDER'S FOOTSTEPS

With fire-lit face, my Faeder's voice
warmed English hearts with songs
of gallant, golden, God-graced, deeds
to right past Danish wrongs.

At Round Head Hill, my Faeder heard
blessed choirs of Saxon bows
scream spite-spiked, sanctifying songs
on vanquished Viking crows.

So onward lads... to Brunanburh
to subdue Satan's threat,
then once more home to warmth and wives,
whilst evil sleeps cold death!

At Wolf's Bane Wood, did Faeder see
a dance of steel-kissed sparks
in frantic flight, to nobly weave
sweet silver, sword-spun arcs,

That met the heads of unblessed filth
and sped their pagan deaths;
their spineless screams encircling all
brave Saxons' final breaths.

So onward lads...to Brunanburh,
for victory's cheer, so loud
that Alfred, stood at God's right hand,
shall burnish deep with pride!

KIMBALL'S PRAYER

For my soul-light Wulfgar; far from wife's warm sight and reach -
should steel-gripped fear rear up on distant fields,
then Thunor's rumbled thunder, born of battle's drums,
could never best my bursting beat of heart,
that roars from home through any fearsome foe
to proudly stand at her noble warrior's arm.
Firm embraced within vow-bound, Saxon shield
breathes your oath for safe return; no mortal blade shall breach.

For Tiw - when war's dice roll to choose which light
next be expunged, behind glazed eyes of hollow sight;
should you view my valiant Wulfgar; seek another trophy death.

For Woden - fairest Lord of Earth and all things hallowed,
observe our Osric; dusk door framed with heart-held tallow;
His Faeder's homeward beacons, lighting hope's path to our hearth.

THE HOPE OF OSRIC

Bright eyes. Wide with love
        Like Faeder's approaching smile
                Reunited hearts

Glossary
Alfred: Iconic Saxon king of England, known as 'Alfred the Great' (849-899).
Brunanburh: English battle in 937, where a Saxon army defeated a combined army of Norse / Scottish /
Irish to unify England. The exact location for the battle is unknown, although it is thought likely to be
somewhere around Cheshire/Lancashire.
Faeder: Anglo-Saxon word for 'father'.
Thunor: Anglo-Saxon God of sky and thunder (comparable to the Norse God, Thor).
Tiw: Anglo-Saxon God of war and combat.
Woden: The chief God of the Anglo-Saxons.

David Hollywood
REPUBLIC OF IRELAND

David's particular interest is in developing a public enthusiasm for poetry among those who aspire to appreciate the genre, but haven't yet made the leap into writing or proclaiming their verse. As a result, he founded, and for several years directed The Colours of Life poetry festivals in Bahrain, and subsequently worked upon the same in Antigua, The West Indies, Ireland and Switzerland, before moving back to Ireland. He is the author of an eclectic collection of poems titled *Waiting Spaces*, plus contributed to *My Beautiful Bahrain, Poetic Bahrain, More of My Beautiful Bahrain* and was the in-house poet for *Bahrain Confidential* magazine and, as a result, he is one of the most widely read Western poets in The Middle East. He is also a regular literary critic for *Taj Mahal Review*, plus an essayist on the subject of poetry appreciation. He has been accredited with membership of The Society of Classical Poets, and has plans for a new collection of poetry and essays to be released shortly.
E: davidhollywood23@hotmail.com

SEND TO END

What slumber is eternity?
If life has chance to send,
A bullet which just once has found,
Its lodgement as your end.

And when you thought the cause was just,
You sacrificed your trust,
In favour of a war that sends,
A young man to his end.

But as within the realms of time,
Just when you're in your prime,
Half-truths through thoughts combined to send,
Your liberty its end.

What futile cause described to send?
You thinking you'd enlist,
Convinced by propaganda's mist,
That war's come to an end.

HAVE A PITY FOR WAR!

Part 1

Have a pity for war,
When its friends are no more.
All its chums gone away,
With no one to slay,
Left silent and calm,
And no one to harm.
It's a destitute life,
In a world without strife!

***

With no conscience to weigh,
Last one killed was today.
Left his life with a moan,
Then poor war made a groan,
As his soul did ascend,
When his breathe came to end.
Wars fates now alone,
With no fighting to own!

If no one is left,
Poor war'll be bereft,
So, let's sanctify peace,
Then we'll breed and increase,
And war'll have no tears,
As we offer our fears,
To his yearning for years,
Of our endless decease.

If there's no one to gore,
Let's invent a new war,
We can kill and be maimed,
In the hope we're reclaimed,
By death who'll ensure,
We live life here no more,
And with choice bits of luck,
By a bullet we're struck.

What worthier cause,
Than addiction to wars?

If our minds are insane,
Then we'll all end the same.
 With no need to abhor,
All the slaughter and gore,
There's an endless extreme,
Of more troops we've forswore.

Give no rest to today,
Case wars friends run away,
With such hunger to feed,
Conflict kills for the need,
Lots of slaughter and more,
Nourished death's by the score.
With no vigour grown old,
Lives are slayed so their cold.

Part 2

What was that terrible moments wrench
that took you from the life you clenched?
At just what time did your desire
end dreams upon that moments pyre?
And as you fell within that trench
did war enlist you with its stench?
Had wagers with the dice of cost
gambled all your days into a frost?

No more to join
with those now lost!
Your life and theirs, purloined at cost,
To all who seeked
or reaped from coin
a fate beyond the line you've crossed,
In countless wars beliefs too meek,
When pitied lives are mocked - then tossed!

History's story's since been sold
of soldiers who with lives paroled,
Escaped their fate, to die, when told!
Did once again through children mould,
An endless list for wars... enrolled!
Conspiring of their youthful plight
to end their joy, which as a right,

Will terminate their lives, with fright!
Enjoying all of conflicts might,

Gives gaze to scope the troops who fight,
Who fall upon the earth forever,
atop the lands their bodies cover,
In search of promised ends that never
give an end to wars endeavour,
Slaughter is the cause retold,
And victories the lie that's sold.

Entombed within conscriptions snares
are our ethics caught in moral scares,
Of causes calls... as war insists,
it's time we stopped our liberal tryst.
We in all conscience should enlist...
... becoming warfare's heroes missed!
When bound by scruples we entrapped,
our principles are then unwrapped.

We say our prayers to God on high,
believing that we'll never die,
We live with thoughts beyond our grave
and never see our tomb engraved.
When life's surrounding warmth is smug,
before we're killed by conflicts hug,
the abstract theories we'd befriend
don't speculate, we'd never end!

Part 3

Do times in times, remind thereof,
the hours spent in thoughts whereof,
we'd go to war for judgements felt,
supporting word's, we'd spouted, spelt?
Offering lives, we see them severed,
Replaced by memories, forever.
Are motives why the peace of dove,
abandons prejudice for love?

***

Make friends with war, and learn to be,
in debt to feuds eternally.
When clinging to our sorrow's woes,
we know we've paid a price that shows,
Conflicts are a 'soul mates' chum,
when beating on their treacherous drum.
They lead us to our death in wars
ensuring voices end in roars.

WAR MEMORIALS

Destruction writes the terms of war,
ensuring rules compete with gore,
When notions nourished seek extreme,
in ideals that neglect esteem,
then as we find a place to kill,
our conscience seeking for the thrill,
all understandings suffer for,
a lack of ethics ruses swore,
were aspirations call for more,
of conquests and a thirst, forswore.

What gallant thoughts determined theme,
are hidden in a peaceful scene?
As troops and victors public trance,
envisioned by our heroes' glance,
towards what history's drummers dance,
now honours for the dead, in this final stance,
brought death to all about perchance,
Believed that hallucinations rant,
was formed of noble reasoned chant,
supporting propagandas cant.

And as we march to cenotaph,
along this nations mournful path,
Towards our memories, of peaceful wrath,
kept sombre by remembrance cask,
We face a judgement on this route,
bout honours through hollow salute,
Acknowledged by the words now mute,
which states whatever cause intent,
was wasteful of the lives now spent,
are arguments disputes repent.

We trudge to honour moments' past,
observing where we can what passed,
Of victory's support which clashed,
with conflicts, for the lives we lost!
And sanctioned through the battle scenes,
 of sculptured portraits killings, cast,
are ideals! That we hold steadfast.
Through views where heroes seem serene,
in battles which their victories mean,

don't show to us - they are obscene!

These monuments preserving scrawl,
depicts endured extremes, enthrals,
our honour for a cause that schemes,
to summon all to duties calls.
Where continents observe with grace,
a praise for us, our kind and race,
whose empires' vast and great, not small,
shall dominate their place and face.
Unless of course they dare not dread,
respect for all of those now dead.

But morals are not weakened by,
an edifice that's imaged thy,
immortal memories of why,
our populations learn to cry.
From centuries of conflicts roar,
that shows the harms the sore have bore,
in ploy's displayed by deeds that stream,
our blood into a plotted scream.
Which domiciles the place we bled,
upon our nations love of red.

Memorials commemorate,
exertions that placate dissent,
When peace which scruples consecrate,
shows gallantry in virtues meant...
to stay the differences, as calls for more,
are aspirations slain by war,
Yet what our talisman of stone has built,
through anniversaries ensigned guilt,
stand useless symbols that evoke,
Our tributes lost, in fights – provoked!

Stephen Gibson

USA

Stephen's latest poetry collection, *Self-Portrait in a Door-Length Mirror*, won the 2017 Miller Williams Prize from the University of Arkansas Press. He has also published six prior collections: *The Garden of Earthly Delights Book of Ghazals* (Texas Review Press, 2016), *Rorschach Art Too* (2014 Donald Justice Prize, Story Line Press, West Chester University), *Paradise* (Miller Williams prize finalist, University of Arkansas Press), *Frescoes* (Lost Horse Press book prize), *Masaccio's Expulsion* (MARGIE/IntuiT House book prize), and *Rorschach Art* (Red Hen Press). He was born and raised in New York City, studied at Syracuse University with W.D. Snodgrass and Philip Booth, and taught for over three decades at Palm Beach State College, before retiring.
E: gibsonwriter@aol.com

CAMPBELL'S SOUP I

Warhol's silkscreen was created half a dozen years
before the Summer of Love in San Francisco,
where my future wife and a girlfriend ran away to

after a former boyfriend was shot down in his helicopter
when she was a senior in high school and didn't know
about Vietnam, body counts, or what was expected of you

at funerals with a boyfriend's blown-up year-book picture
and another of him in uniform - his parents (in front row)
who also didn't know what they were supposed to do -

but everyone in time learning, it being repeated over and over
like cans of soup.

FEAR THE WALKING DEAD

They're all still out there in those rice paddies,
all still trying to control their water buffaloes
that want to run off in any direction, instead

being kept in line despite our hillside artillery,
from where my friend watches them explode -
that's what my friend says out at dinner: drafted

at nineteen, then boot camp, then in-country
where he doesn't know his ass from his elbow
(he knows now he's bi-polar and takes his meds) -

not George Romero's movie zombies, the zombies
in his head.

Kath Boyle
VIETNAM/ENGLAND

Kathleen Boyle (nee Dodd), was born in Liverpool, England, where she spent her childhood years before leaving to train as a teacher in Hull in 1972. Kathleen has worked as a teacher in Hull, Leeds, London and Carlisle, and at international schools in Colombia, Bahrain, Cairo, Armenia and Vietnam. She has written stories and poems throughout her life, and published a collection of poems about growing up in 1950s Liverpool entitled, *Sugar Butties and Mersey Memoirs*, as well as a collection of poems for children about a teddy bear called *Harry Pennington*. During her time in Bahrain she wrote *The Pearl House*, a short story which spans the cultural divides of Liverpool and Bahrain. The story, together with her poems, *Bahrain* and *Umm Al Hassam*, were published in the collections; *My Beautiful Bahrain* and *More of My Beautiful Bahrain*. Kathleen has written a series of children's stories for Beirut publishers Dar El Fikr, two of which, *The Jewel of the Deep* and *The Magic Pearl and Dilmun*, have now been illustrated and published. Kathleen has also contributed to the poetry and short prose collections, *Love, Travel, Lonely* and *Happy*. In 2015, while teaching in Cairo, Kathleen published her novella, *Catherine of Liverpool* and completed a revision and Part 2 of the story during her years in Armenia, where she was Head of Primary at CIS Armenia. A mother of three and grandmother of two, with a home in Cotehill, Cumbria, she has given author presentations in Russia, Armenia, Vietnam and Liverpool. She is currently teaching at SIS Binh Duong in Vietnam, where she has recently finished her latest book *The Storyteller of Cotehill Wood*.
E: kathdodd@aol.com

THE CHILDREN

We were the children
who roamed the
bomb sites
and listened
to stories of
our parents'
war.

We were the children of
pick up the pieces
and mend so we'll
somehow forget.
The children of
shell-shocked
and war-torn;
of rations,
and heartache;
of rebuild and
make-do;
of hope.

Tracy Davidson
ENGLAND

Tracy is British and lives in Warwickshire, and writes poetry and flash fiction. Her work has appeared in various publications and anthologies including: *Poet's Market, Mslexia, Atlas Poetica, Modern Haiku, The Binnacle, A Hundred Gourds, Shooter, Artificium, Journey to Crone, The Great Gatsby Anthology, Aftermath: Explorations of Loss and Grief, WAR* and *In Protest: 150 Poems for Human Rights.*
E: james0309@btinternet.com

THE FORGOTTEN ONES

Orphans. Maimed ones. Not the pretty able-bodied ones
celebrities fly half-way round the world to adopt.

A little girl makes her way outside on makeshift crutches,
her left leg gone, right foot amputated, the leg
ending in a misshapen ugly stump.

It looks red and sore. She hasn't got used to the crutches yet,
and they're a little short, so her stump keeps bumping the ground.
Infection is likely to set in. She might lose more.

A teenage boy, so nearly – but not quite – a man, stares moodily
across the yard. Both legs gone, one arm hanging lifeless at his side.
He watches the other boys play football. Playing as best they can
with their various combinations of missing and mangled limbs,
one who's sightless but follows the ball through sound,
another with shrapnel lodged deep in his brain. It will work
its way through until it kills him. But he's smiling now
and whooping, daydreaming of the World Cup.

A charity worker comes to the door to watch, needing a break
from nursing those too sick to play.
She blinks back tears, trying to forget the baby boy,
just four months old, who died in her arms during the night.
She hasn't been here long enough to harden her heart
and accept that sometimes death is kinder.
An ambulance enters the compound, making her look up
and the children pause in their games.
Two stretchers are lifted out, the thin blood-soaked
blankets showing what parts are missing beneath.

The nurse sighs and calls to her colleagues, break over,
and wonders for the umpteenth time: "When will it end?"

First appeared in *In Protest: 150 Poems for Human Rights* anthology in 2013.

AFTERMATH - SADRIYA DISTRICT, BAGHDAD

After the blast...an eerie silence, just for a minute...
then the screaming starts.

Smoke clears enough for survivors - with ringing ears
and watering eyes - to see what their local market has become.

A sea of red and grey - blood and debris
surrounding piles of bodies, parts of bodies,
hunks of burnt flesh.

The stench unmistakeable, nothing else
in the world smells like it, or as bad.

Soldiers arrive, try to clear the way
for ambulances to approach.
Locals clamber over the carnage, looking for loved ones.

A teenage boy calls for his mother and sister,
slipping and sliding in the bloody remains of his neighbours.
He finds his mother's shopping bag, the one she made herself
from scraps of material cut up from their old baby clothes.
Her hand is still clutching it, but her face is gone.
His wail is heard and echoed across the city.

A young American soldier, not much older than the boy,
stops and tries to offer comfort.

The boy turns on him, shock and grief
replaced by anger, hate. Pointing at the soldier

he screams his rage and frustration, wanting someone
to take it out on. Someone to blame.

The soldier stands and takes it, blinking back tears of his own,
understanding the meaning if not the actual words.

The boy's voice gives out, the anger drains away,
at last he slumps, defeated, into the soldier's outstretched arms.

The boy's father comes, gently extracts his son, holds him close,
nods gratitude to the soldier, mumbles: "Thank you",

the limit of his English. The soldier nods back,
looks around at the vision of hell, and thinks: "For what?"

A FATHER'S LAMENT

I am a father
who could not protect his child
from the pain of war.

>She complains of pins
>and needles in legs
>no longer there.

I am a father
who stands by impotently
while his daughter cries.

>She asks me to scratch
>her left foot, relieve the itch
>she insists she feels.

I am a father
who knows her life will never
be the same again.

>She was told the truth
>but shrapnel in her brain plays
>with her memory.

I am a father
who feels shame at thinking she'd
be better off dead.

>I pretend to scratch,
>my fingers fanning the air
>way beneath her stump.

I am a father
who knows though peace is declared
her battle remains.

>With eyes closed, she smiles
>and doesn't notice the tears
>rolling down my cheek

THE DESERTER

When he wakes, he knows it's for the last time.
Knows that this will be the day the bullets
rip through his chest, break his unworthy heart.
He feels too sick for his meagre breakfast,
throat too tight to swallow cloudy water.
He dresses, no medals on his jacket,
bare hanging threads where the stripes used to be.
He prays to God, though he doesn't believe.

They come for him at first light. It is time.
All is silence, no birdsong to break it,
no chattering voices, no friendly face,
only the blank looks of war-weary men.
He feels the pole at his back, the rough rope,
the blindfold, and then... just blessed darkness.

First published online by *Strong Verse* in 2015.

Bill Cushing

USA

Named in honour of a Union Civil War Naval officer, Bill Cushing was born in Virginia when his own father was serving on submarines. He lived in various parts of the United States as well as the Virgin Islands and Puerto Rico, before moving to California. Returning to college after his own service in the Navy and working on ships, he was called the 'blue collar poet' by classmates at the University of Central Florida. He then earned an MFA in writing from Goddard College. He taught college English at colleges in the Los Angeles area. His writing has been published in numerous newspapers, magazines, journals, and anthologies, both in print and online. Bill's current project, *Notes and Letters*, combines poetry with music, and is on both Facebook and YouTube. He has two books of poetry available; *A Former Life* and *Music Speaks*.

E: piscespoet@yahoo.com

DROWNING IN RETREAT IN 1991

With the battle lost, those few who
survived buried themselves

under sand, dug in only to get
bulldozed beneath a front stretching

across 170 miles
of parched shoreline. Did these Iraqi

sons and fathers, pawns praying
to Allah, beg or shout for mercy

over the thrum of diesel engines
like surf drumming in the desert.

What god could've heard the screams
of these conscripts coming from

under those granular waves?
All noise is muffled as throats and lungs

filled with that smothering tide.
Their blood, seeping into the grains,

makes its own mud, and they -
the men never really wanting

to be there - fall victim to this,
a new and unintended assault.

First published in *Roll Call: Days of War* (Canada: October 2019).

A SONNET TO SLAUGHTER

The ground held no value, the town little use,
except for foot-rotted,grey-clad men
hoping to find much-needed shoes.
What followed was beyond their ken
when groves of peach trees and fields of wheat
became hallowed witness to brutalities
as lice-ridden troops, bound for defeat,
charged over meadows and fallen bodies.
The banshee wail of the rebel yell
arose with bayonets and shot lead;
cannonade shook buildings,roof tiles fell,
and after three days, desperation led
Gettysburg, then a place of little worth -
now one of lost causes, "a perfect hell on earth."

Inspired by the diary of Robert H. Carter, private: 22nd Massachusetts infantry. First published in *Roll Call: Days of War* (Canada: October 2019). Helen Shaible Annual Sonnet Competition: third place (United States).

WAR TO END

Expectant delight of carnage raised their blood.
Calvary and infantry mixed with tanks and machine guns for
the "justice of our cause:" Romantic notions of war,
Temporary trenches deepen to the thud
of incessant music of artillery caissons landed and tore
through the men hunkered down in others' blood.
A lattice-work worming through fields, reinforced with planks of two-
by-four,
ordinance and flowers grow out of moss and mud.
Makeshift pyramids of bones and skulls grow before
trails of barbed wire meant to impede and lessen *esprit d'corps.*
Housing for ammo boxes and corpses, fed by flesh, irrigated by
blood.
Ghosts of gas-blinded and limbless men fall for
the war to end all wars: prelude to more and bigger wars.

First published in *Poetry 24* (United Kingdom: December 2018).

Bernadette Perez
USA

"What I create today is who I am at this moment. If my art can touch one soul, save one life, touch one heart then my craft has conveyed it's message." In 1990, Bernadette received the Silver Poet Award from World of Poetry. Her work has appeared in *The Wishing Well; Musings* (2010), *Small Canyons* (2013) and in *Poems 4 Peace* (2014). Contribution to *La Familia: La Casa de Colores*, and *Fix and Free* anthologies. Winner of the Wagner Society of Santa Fe Audience Favourite: *Write Your Own Prize Song.* Included in the mega-unity poem by Juan Felipe. Included in *The Americans Museum Inscription* by Shinpei Takeda. Published in over 100 publications between 2015-2019.
E: bpburritos@aol.com

BROKEN SILENCE

The battle - no one knows

Blurted out in anger
You don't know

Buried secrets

Through the Devil's lens
A mother's nightmare
I barely sleep these days
I blame myself

It's hard to comprehend
The pain is unreal

Evil monsters
I can't stand you
I hate you
You F___N piece of S**t

Invade my home
Harm my Family
Take their innocence

How dare you

Anger unexplainable
Wrath of rage hostile
Some may view this as emotion
I trigger this a response

I do not know where to begin
I do not know where this will end

My intention is not to forgive
We can't forget
I now hate for you to live

To know hate the way I do
No one can fathom

The depth of forgiveness is not mine to give

The thought of the children
Is tearing my heart out

Ask me again tomorrow
My answer is the same

My very thoughts scare me to death
I toss
I turn
I walk the halls

To hold you tightly in my arms
Protect you
Never leave your side

I did not know
I might as well have been blind
I hate myself for being naïve
I hate myself for being stupid

Back to you
I don't know what to do
I listen
We cry
I hold you
I never want to let you go
For in my arms you are safe
Do not let secrets haunt you
Release the evil

Grieving and healing is slow
Some days you just don't care
It seems to go on forever
There are days I am mad, angry and hurt
There are days I feel I failed
Days of deep downfall

Then I remember - Love
We have each other
These Monsters can go to hell

Barbara Hawthorn
NEW ZEALAND

Barbara lives in Auckland, New Zealand. She is a retired teacher (Mathematics) with a lifelong addiction to writing. Currently a member of International Writers' Workshop, Northcote, New Zealand, Barbara is a musician, playing mandola in The Auckland Mandolinata Orchestra.

E: john.hawthorn@xtra.co.nz

IT HAPPENED RIGHT HERE

It can hardly be called a tourist attraction,
And yet somehow one is compelled to go.
And it was all quite jovial on the coach...
Strangers yesterday, strangers tomorrow,
Locked today on the same path,
Blurred background figures in each other's photos,
Clutching guidebooks in whatever language.
And here was the spot – this very place...
Our tour leader was efficient, had all the statistics,
Delivered without outrage, then turned us loose,
To drift numb In the torrent of guided chatter.
          Why did I come?
Except there was Grandpa's voice in my ear,
The way his voice would break when he spoke,
Of 1945 and what he found here. What did I expect to find,
                    All these years later?
          It was the eyes that pierced me in the end...
                    Displays of faded grey photos,
          Herded   they stood   threatened   bewildered,
          Questions unspoken on their lips...
          Why us? What are we doing on this page?
                    Who is writing this history book?
And I had no answers – even all these years later.

It was quieter on the coach returning –
Some slept,
     Some checked their travel plans...
Tomorrow?... what flight? - indeed what country?
          Meanwhile in the back seat,
          Half a world from home,
Even as I planned the afternoon's sightseeing,
          I squirmed to remember
          Blood-splattered sites of shame,
                    On my own soil.
Where I have never stood in regretful homage.

BRACING FOR A BOMB
(Baghdad 2002)

Talks it seems have broken down
        No chance of negotiation
        The next step they say... but they don't say
        Rumours just out of reach – whispers fly
        Like desert dust in a once blue sky.
We wait. What else can we do?

Summer rolls on,
        Air heavy-scented with the roses on the wall
Overlaid now   with a whiff of panic.
I shall prune back those roses before the war begins
It's too early but I cannot bear the thought
        Of red petals pooling in the courtyard
        The image is too strong;
        Should this peaceful courtyard turn to rubble
        Let the devastation lie open to the camera's eye,
        Not left to hide
        Beneath a coverlet of roses running wild.
I shall cut them back, the buds before their time
And full blown heads basking now in their prime
        And the delirium of bees.

The truth is... I don't know what else to do;
Water I have stored in all the pots
        Honey and cheese   candles and oil
        Dates, dried figs   a little wine
        Precious handfuls of flour –
The markets are quite empty now
Blankets and bandages I have laid by... just in case
        The young ones we have sent away
- Allah be merciful – to some safer place

So come my dear. We have done all we can.
Look, I have coffee made. Set out those petal-thin cups
Seldom used.   Here in the courtyard I have spread
A rug beneath the roses on the wall
        This is almost the last of the coffee
        Savour it   Sip by sip.
Then I will wash the cups tenderly
Put them back on the shelf
That same shelf which shakes

When tanks rumble by.
                        - I tremble too
Then I will cut back the roses. What else can I do?

THE RETURN

When Dad came back from war
We took a taxi down to the wharf,
- the ship already loomed tall above -
Gaped at the soldiers crowding the rail
Cheering and waving, punching the air.
            And one of them is my Dad.
So we hugged the one Mum said was him
All scooped together in a too-tight bear hug
His head burrowed in mum's shoulder -
            We could feel him shaking -
Weren't expecting a Dad who cried,
            When Dad came back, came back from war.

When Dad came back from war
He got himself a dog - jet black Labrador -
Called him Red – go figure –
I didn't name him for his colour, he said
Red was a good mate, a good mate...
            A sentimental man was my Dad.
We stayed with Granny quite a lot that year,
Heaven knows, they need to catch up
Sort themselves out, she'd say, and you two
            Would jangle anyone's nerves.
Stayed there heaps too when little Joey-Mack was born
            When Dad came back, came back from war.

When Dad came back from war,
He reckoned we were running wild
Reined us in with the flat of his hand
And a roar like thunder.
            A hard man was my Dad
We almost wished he had not come back –
Oh no, no, never that. But all the same
We much preferred him in the photo frame
        Safely behind glass, smeared
With four years' worth of goodnight-Daddy kisses,
            But Dad came back, came back from war.

When Dad came back from war
He couldn't stand our tea-time chatter
Lurched up from the table with a groan
Took his plate and sat on the porch,

Fed most of it to Red.
        A rake thin man was my Dad.
Joey-Mack would slide from his high-chair
Toddle to stand between Dad's knees
        Leave them alone, Mum said
Set us to drying the dishes. Quietly, she said.
        When Dad came back, came back from war.

        I saw a photo once. Dad squatting on his heels
        Beside a fearsome tank with his mates -
        Dad with Joe and Mack and freckle-faced Red -
        Just four boys, really. But only one came back:
        No, none of those boys made it back, he said
        A broken man was my Dad.
He could laugh well enough, cradling a beer in his hand
On Fridays down at the RSA. But he'd come back brooding
Go darkly to bed. Never wanted to talk about war.
        What's to say? War is a waste
Kept his medals hidden in his underwear drawer,
When Dad came back, came back from war.

This poem refers to Horst Bienek, a Polish poet, arrested by the Russians at the age of seventeen, as a member of the Polish underground. Sentenced to twelve years in a Siberian prison camp. He wrote about war for the rest of his life. I admired him. We were much the same age – but what different lives!

Chrys Salt
ENGLAND/SCOTLAND

Chrys is a seasoned performer and a widely published and anthologized poet. She has performed in festivals across the UK in Europe, America, Canada, Finland and India, and written in almost every genre except the novel. Numerous awards include a National Media Award, an Arts and Business Award, Several Writing Bursaries and a Fringe First from The Edinburgh Festival. She has published seven books for actors (Pub: Methuen Drama) and nine poetry collections (publishers various). Her poem *The Burning* was selected as one of the Best Scottish Poems 2012. Her pamphlet *Weaver of Grass* was shortlisted for the Callum MacDonald Memorial Award. Her most recent collection, *The Punkawallah's Rope* is rooted in a trip to India in 2015 to appear at The Kolkata Literary Festival. She received a Creative Scotland Bursary in 2017 to research material in The Yukon for her forthcoming collection about the Klondike Gold Rush. She was The International Poet at the Tasmanian Poetry Festival in 2019. In 2014 Chrys was awarded an MBE in the Queen's Birthday Honours List for Services to The Arts. She is Artistic Director of BIG LIT: The Stewartry Book Festival, a five day literary festival in SW Scotland now in its ninth year.
E: chrys@chryssalt.com
W: www.chryssalt.com
W: www.biglit.org

I AM NOT ANGRY...

I am not angry with the sun.
It can't be blamed
for lighting up the tumbling stars
of the magnolia, and
polishing the evergreens -
on this day of all days
when families in lorries
cars and donkey carts,
flee from their frightened cities,
her blistering sister on their backs.

I am not angry with the Spring.
It does not mean
to open like a box of paints –
splashing japonica and daffodil
down all the neighbouring gardens
on this day of all days -
the Tigris rocked on her anchor
from Baghdad to Nineveh
and the bomb-shocked sky
blooming with deadlier flowers.

I am not angry with the earth.
It can't avoid
rebirth - delivering
greening March on sprung beds
of last year's leaf-mould
on this day of all days
when sons, fresh killed
go home in body bags
to lie forever under it
in Devon villages. Iraqi sands.

MISSING

As soon as he could walk
he'd abseil down the cot side –
pad in low-slung pyjamas
down the corridor to hide.
She'd hunt and call - alarmed
at first - then it became a nightly ritual,
a game, with him unharmed,
chuckling his guttural
chuckle when I found
him in his wicker toy-basket
gone to ground
with soldier, tank and rabbit -
or holed up in his duvet –
keeping cave with Marmite
baited breath – primed to waylay
mewith bombardments of delight.

Now I can't find him anywhere.
My care unplugged, the Ariel
of my sixth sense 'off air.'
He's lost, gone AWOL
from my mothering radar.
I scan photographs, unpick
the tabloid propaganda -
the multi-media rhetoric -
fillet the news analysis
for clues. Pray for a sighting
of him on a dusty road, his
Battery delivering aid - not fighting!
I magnify the map.
The names of foreign town and street
are anagrams I can't unwrap
his camouflage - complete.

SEASCAPE

A pair of squalllng gannets scuff the beach
The sun, a pale balloon is out of reach
and the summer child who had it tight
walks with his mother in the dimming light
towards the safe sea wall -

... and beyond the long horizon –
men, massing with their guns.
Fathers, husbands, boyfriends, lovers -

other mother's sons.

A turn-tail tide runs out and drops her shawl
of froth and weed. A milk-eyed mackerel
lost from a fisher's evening haul
lolls like a lazy bather in a pool
under the safe sea-wall -

... and beyond the long horizon –
men, massing with their guns.
Fathers, husbands, boyfriends, lovers -

other mother's sons.

An open page of sand blurs to peach-bloom
scribbled with graffiti of the sand-worm
and the scatty hieroglyphs of feet
of child and seabird on its fading sheet
under the safe sea wall.

I read in jetsam war's lunatic symbols -
the shingle's bone-screed; sucking crab-holes
burying the living, arms of trees,
boat-shard, sheep hull – carnage of savage seas
under the safe sea wall

... and beyond the long horizon –
men, massing with their guns.
Fathers, husbands, boyfriends, lovers
Fathers, husbands, boyfriends, lovers
Fathers, husbands, boyfriends, lovers
                              and other mother's sons.

John Grey
USA/AUSTRALIA

John is an Australian poet, US resident. Recently published in *Hawaii Pacific Review, Dalhousie Review* and *Qwerty,* with work upcoming in *Blueline, Willard and Maple* and *Clade Song*.
E: jgrey5790@gmail.com

JOE, HOME FROM THE BATTLE

He reckoned war for a fool's game.
No way he could both see it through
and come out alive.
Fate he could deal with.
But not when it involved crazy men
who couldn't speak English.
He chopped off three fingers.
The army sent him home.
His wife called him a coward and
went back to her mother.

He was competing with his own dead body
and the corpse won.
His drinking buddies gave him the cold shoulder also.
He'd plant himself at a table
in the corner of his neighbourhood bar,
retreat into his beers.

Looking after an apartment house
all by himself proved difficult.
He swore that in the next war,
he'd amputate his left hand.
But he never could cook a damn anyhow,
even with all digits intact.

Finding work wasn't easy.
The army was no help.
To them, he was coward first class.
He took to begging
accompanied by a sign that read,
"Homeless vet."
One guy gave him a buck
and said, "You have my gratitude."
He overpaid.

I heard that he tried to shoot himself
but he could barely hold the gun,
only managed to graze his skull.
He was committed to a sanatorium.
Tap tap (silence) (silence) (silence)
Tap tap (silence((silence) (silence)
That's him.

BRIAN'S WAR

Brian says he wakes up at one or two a.m.
with the story in his head.
It lives there. It only comes out at night.
He shakes. He sweats.
His wife would roll over in disgust.
Then she rolled over one last time,
right out of his life.

The scene shifts.
Sometimes it's Vietnam, early seventies.
Then it's Afghanistan, just this past year.
Jungle or desert? The background's all a blur.

Small children play outside a shack.
An older boy gathers wood.
Another whittles.
Their mother hangs washing.
Brian's with some soldiers,
looking for the man of the house
who's probably Cong or an insurgent
or Taliban or something.
They just need to grab hold of someone
and shake it out of him.

He grasps the eldest by the arm.
"My father's gone," the boy says.
Something crazy happens.
The kid threatens with his whittling knife.
One of the troop shoots him with a pistol.
He falls dead and bloody in Brian's arms.
The mother screams then gathers up
the others, runs with them, still screaming
into the hut.
With their firepower, Brian's men could
raze that hovel in an instance.
Weapons are aimed but no triggers pulled.
Brian's still holding the dead kid in his arms.
He's trembling but the corpse is calm and warm.
One of the men peels the boy off him,
drops it to the ground.
Brian takes command.
"There's no one here. Let's go."

That's where it always ends, he says.
It takes him forever to go to back to sleep.

He wonders about what the dead boy
would have become,
what scars still burn the skin of the survivors.
And who were his men looking for anyhow?
Did their quarry even exist?

Brian was never in the military
though he's seen a lot of movies,
watches the news faithfully.
Nothing goes smooth for him in ordinary life.
He can just imagine what would happen
in extreme circumstances.
But he doesn't have to imagine.
Extreme circumstances do it for him.

His buddy Cole has been in war
and he sleeps well.
"Did you ever kill anyone?" asks Brian.
over his third beer, Cole's first.
"Nobody you'd know," answers Cole.
He's wrong there.

Alicja Maria Kuberska
POLAND

Alicja Maria is an award winning Polish poet, novelist, journalist and editor. She is a member of the Polish Writers Associations in Warsaw, and IWA Bogdani, Albania. She is also a member of the directors' board of the Soflay Literature Foundation, Our Poetry Archive (India) and Cultural Ambassador for Poland (Inner Child Press, USA). Her poems have been published in numerous anthologies and magazines in Poland, Czech Republic, Slovakia, Hungary, Belgium, Bulgaria, Albania, Spain, the UK, Italy, the USA, Canada, Argentina, Chile, Peru, Israel, Turkey, India, Uzbekistan, South Korea, Taiwan, Australia, South Africa, Zambia, and Nigeria. She received two medals - the Nosside UNESCO Competition in Italy (2015), and European Academy of Science Arts and Letters in France (2017). She also received a reward from the Italian international literary competition: Tra le parole e 'elfinito (2018). She was announced the poet of 2017 by Soflay Literature Foundation (2018), and has also received the Bolesław Prus Prize Poland (2019), Culture Animator Poland (2019) and first prize Premio Internazionale di Poesia Poseidonia- Paestrum Italy (2019).
E: alicja107@vp.pl

WAR IN THE MIDDLE EAST

Memories like grains of sand,
during a storm in the desert,
swirl violently in the mind.
They hit hard, hurt badly.

Eye wanders around a desolate city
I remember, a school was there
and next to it a library and a flower shop.
Huge cavities in the ground gape instead
surrounded by charred tree stumps.

Silence spills in a wide stream
over empty streets and ashes,
settling like dust on broken glass.
Birds flew away, the absent inhabitants fell silent.
Wind wails among the ruins and then,
as echo, the whistle of falling bombs returns.

In a surviving building without a wall,
as if on a great theatrical stage of life,
an old man sits alone, reading a book.
Hunger and fear drove neighbours away
He did not run, and became a guardian of hope

Poor people suffer and die.
Politicians speak beautifully of peace,
democracy, and human rights.
Greedy businessmen count profits
from the trade of weapons.

Vampires hover over the oil fields
swabbing the last drops of black blood
from the tormented desert land.

CRYING ANGEL

I saw an angel in my dream,
as he turned his tear-stained face.

Love burned at the stake.
Hatred set the fire.
Its stinging tongues
annihilated goodness and mercy.
The ashes of hopes and dreams fell down,
they turned into grey dust.
Nothing was left but pain
and suffering of the survivors.

Fear lived in the ruins of the abandoned houses.
Despair played on the cello
a long, whining melody,
or maybe it was just the wind,
which howled and whirled.
It blew away along the empty streets
the paper tears of torn books.
It opened widely
the mutilated windows and the doors,
leading to nowhere.

Silence – the companion of death,
muted the complaints in the dead mouths.
Delicate and fragile human bodies
returned to the earth.
They turned to dust.
The grass healed the wounds
- the deep craters left by bombs,
The compassionate rains washed them gently.

The moon, like an enormous pendulum,
told the time and measured vanishing.

John-Karl Stokes
AUSTRALIA

John-Karl is internationally known as one of Australia's most daring and interesting of poets and librettists. He's on a campaign to bring back plain-speaking to the most emotional writings in English.

E: johnstokespoet@me.com
W: www.JohnKarlStokes.com

BRONZE WALL WITH FALSE FLOWERS

We burnt our own sons
and daughters, having failed
in our efforts to circumvent
war, the enemy

They, whom we feel beyond
who won't be found
can't hear us
or reach this bronzed
skin, or stroke of
our imagined bells

We, the accidentally born
have missed our chance
to sing them... denied
their echo, their cry
in lightning, sharp
as certain darkness

When the names crowd in
When the drum's heart is
silenced by a leaving
grant we, too, can look
beyond a cold doorway:
the never-touching

and not shrink back
The river continues
one drop, one day
at a time, one love:
the mother country
and her harsh rebuke...
accepted

and the red, last
flower darkening

National War Memorial.

Kathleen Bleakley
AUSTRALIA

Kathleen has four published poetry and prose collections: *Azure* (2017), *Lightseekers*, photography by 'pling (2015), *jumping out of cars*, with Andrea Gawthorne, images by 'pling, (2004), and *Passionfruit & Other Pieces*, with prints by Hannah Parker (1995). Kathleen's poetry has been widely published in literary journals including internationally. Kathleen has a Bachelor of Creative Arts (Double Major Creative Writing & English Literature, with Distinction) from the University of Wollongong, Australia. Kathleen lives with her celestial, twin star – in life and art – 'pling, between the escarpment and the sea, in Wollongong.
E: kathleen@pling.id.au
W: www.Ginninderrapress.org.au/poetry

SUICIDE BOMBER

I wake from a dream
of meeting Fatima
shopping for her last supper
at a Casablanca souk
she's selecting
the greenest vegetables
halal meat
succulent dates
honey cakes
a feast for her family
my parting gift she explains
holding my gaze
searching her deep-set olive eyes
I ask *where are you going?*
yet knowing
she says tomorrow *I'll be with Allah*
wanting to stop her
wanting to halt the world
with ideas contaminated
as mad cow disease
I offer *please, you are precious*

Previously published in: *Muse*, Canberra's Arts Monthly; *The Canberra Times; jumping out of cars*, and *Lightseekers*, both published by Ginninderra Press, and in *WAR* by Collections of Poetry and Prose.

ASH GARDEN

Turning the pages of an ash garden
The Battle for Baghdad 2003

Hiroshima 1945: flesh no longer belongs to bodies
lying in American hospitals

The Gulf War 1991/how quickly action is named/a new computer
game

Acid rains, the garden grows heads without names, a thousand
origami cranes

Charcoal rings around garden beds
promises break & fall in an autumn park
a bronzed arm
on the mantle of peace
golden gifts for the victor

A blackened wall, sixty thousand poppies scattered
the fallen ones, where is the unknown civilian?

These children have suitcases
Gas masks are abandoned
The scent of rosemary & thyme
branding our memory cells

Turn singed pages of an ash garden
we are fed the news, too full to remember
John Wayne gallops into the latest ad break

People behind desks getting fatter/bellies distend
hunger shrieks
children trying to run
not enough water in the desert storm

Sing me a lull-a-lie
stumbling in the halls of forgetting
too dark to read in the ash garden

Previously published in: *Muse, Canberra's Arts* Monthly; *The Canberra Times*; *Lightseekers*, and *First Refuge*, poems on social justice – both published by Ginninderra Press and in *WAR* by Collections of Poetry and Prose.

David A Banks
ENGLAND

David escaped from the confines of academic writing and now roams the fresh pastures of poetry and theatre, where he encounters far less bull. He regularly earwigs on conversations in a number of café haunts under the guise of 'research'. When not reading or writing, he has been known to make wooden dolls' houses, manufacture interesting pieces of firewood on a lathe, or spend many hours in the garden planning what he might do next time the weather conditions are absolutely perfect. He lives by the wise words of a respected friend who advised that most work activities should be given 'a good coat of looking-at' before commencing.
E: traveldab@gmail.com

SOUNDS OF CONFLICT

The farmer pointed towards the concrete structure
"Kilnsea sound mirror they call it"
"World War One device to listen for incoming airships."

"You heard something strange?" he said.
The young man nodded a tousled head

He had balanced atop the iron post
at the focus of the mirror and heard distant cries
that grew steadily louder until he was shaken from his roost.

The farmer sighed and stroked his jaw
"Folk heard noises there during the Great War,

and again before the second world war,
and before each and every war that followed
... and now it seems it's back again."

As he walked away he turned and said with sorrow
"Go home young man, and prepare for tomorrow."

Kilnsea Sound Mirror: an acoustic sound mirror built during WW1 near Hull, UK

Bill Cox
SCOTLAND

Bill was born in Aberdeen, Scotland, where he still lives. He started writing in 2014 and won the 2016/17 One Giant Read flash fiction competition. He has had work published in a number of anthologies and online. He describes his writing as 'inspiring and transcendent', but then he would say that, wouldn't he?
E: malphesius@yahoo.com
Blog: northeastnotesblog.wordpress.com

HIS PATRIOTIC DUTY

The General

The General stands over the table,
Uniform starched, belt buckle gleaming,
Surveying the battlefield in miniature.
He moves the regiments hither and thither,
Thousands of men reduced to wooden markers.
As they manoeuvre smoothly across the map
The General nods his head in quiet satisfaction.
Later, orders given, he sits in silent contemplation,
Sipping his brandy, puffing on his cigar.
One eye on the clock, he fancies that, perhaps,
He can hear the artillery barrage begin in the distance.
Raising his glass in salute, he thinks to himself,
Good show, our valiant Tommies.
Then he retires to bed, sleeping soundly till the morn,
When, once more, he will arise
And do his patriotic duty.

The Soldier

The soldier stands shivering in the trench,
Uniform shabby and torn, belly rumbling, boots muddy.
He looks at his comrades,
Poor souls from the slums like him,
Stamping their feet in the evening cold.
At the appointed hour the whistles blast, the ladders go up,
The artillery begins its covering barrage.
Resigning himself to his fate, the soldier climbs the rungs
And steps into no-man's land, his fellow Tommies at his side.
Together they march forward
Into withering machine-gun fire.
In the midst of this industrial slaughter
The soldier is struck
And falls,
Never to rise again,
His patriotic duty done.

THE LIGHT OF MY LIFE

You burn brighter than the sun;
A radiant supernova brought to earth.
Your touch expands across the spaces of my life.
The places that created me,
Nurtured me,
Erased by your terrible, furious glory.
Your power shapes my destiny,
Scorching me through the decades,
A life lived in your shadow,
A death by your lethal caress.
All this arises from that moment,
That infinitesimal yet all-encompassing time,
When I looked upon your unforgiving beauty.
I stood, transfixed, as your cataclysmic love
Burst forth from its metal womb,
That sleepy August morning,
In the skies,
Over the city
Of my birth;
Hiroshima.

John Tunaley
ENGLAND

Born in Manchester in 1945 (father; foundry hand, mother; crane-driver), John now lives in Robin Hoods' Bay, North Yorkshire. He's in a few writing groups plus a painting group... a tai-chi group... a music group... his French class... then there's Open Gardens to help sort out for every June (proceeds to the Alzheimer's Society), and the grandchildren who demand he plays with them…. he gets no rest. He enjoys the 'anthology' approach, and tends to stick to sonnets as the form exercises some control over his worse excesses.
E: johntunaley@yahoo.co.uk

THE BATTLE FOR POLAND
(September 1st, 1939)

Border Village Before the Storm

The furnace grew hotter; roaring louder
as the bellows operators (muscles
and sinews cracking), increased their efforts.
At the heart of the fire lay a stone egg...
black as coal to begin with, it changed as
the temperature rose. Through midnight-blue to
iridescent peacock...fluorescent gold
followed by glowing yellow...then blind-white...

Twice before it had been quenched. First in snake -
oil, then in cockerels' blood. This time, a
claw footed iron bath brim-full with the
shaman's magic liquid was to be tried.
Nothing... we threw it on the dung heap. Weeks later
the village idiot brought us the broken shell...

AQUITAINE 1944 - THE RESISTANCE

Two Nights Past Full Moon

In far corners of the cemetery
the machine-gun chatters away… 'It's your
own fault'… 'You've only yourselves to blame'… then…
'Resistance is futile, you should know that'…

What with bringing the cows in for milking,
drawing water from the well and oil-lamps
to be lit; just carrying on life as
normal is difficult enough for us.

Eventually, the soldiers will melt
away into the darkness, the human
bonfire collapse into cooling ashes.
A waning moon will shine on the village.

As they have done over millennia,
Wild things will come to rake through the remains.

Eftichia Kapardeli
GREECE

Dr. Eftichia has a Doctorate from Arts and Culture World Academy. Born in Athens and lives in Patras, she writes poetry, stories, short stories, xai-kou, essays and novels. She studied journalism AKEM (Athenian training centre), University of Cyprus in Greek culture. She has many awards in national competitions, and is a member of the IWA and The World Poets Society, and has contributed to a number of international poetry collections.
E: kapardeli@gmail.com
FB: @kapardeli.eftichia

CORONA VIRUS

The human body is fragile
with an invisible enemy
that in death
every day leads it

Oh! Mother Nature is sacred
how cruel and ugly I was
we have treated you
we the People
without wisdom and logic
we hurt you without guilt
Let's breathe fresh air
let us walk in your virgin paths again
and don't leave us in the terrible
our actions

Oh! mother Nature
Your magic hug and that
let the only "breath" remain forever
on earth a unique our companion

REQUIEM OF SILENCE

Voices, dates and
names full of expectations
In piles of flowers
of a generation, the past
the crystal precious tears
I close the circles
in the fires of the earth stones

PRISONERS OF WAR

Nuclear kisses
with a thousand tongues of fire
Prisoners of war
Rain, mud, hunger
beatings and
that gardenia
that has fallen to the ground
from wounded hands
dripping red blood
Endless piles
transformed into one
infinite human mass
without sensations
without form and meaning
Little life, thousands of chills
and their own body
immersed in sleep
in a closed yellow shell
hiding in the soil

WAR

The tops of the mountain
the secret sun is resting,
and the rays, souls like flames
jump out of the war
the fire

Heroic hearts
soldiers with bayonets
in the hands, they fight
The helmets rolled quietly
hair, torn legs, mouths
who were silenced by the wind
the naked cries

Opposite the sun
new blood flows
Amaranth blossoms the earth embraces
when the skies open
the immortal heroes, he wakes up

On the battle front, he secretly invites them
bodies with immobile hands
white breasts on all breasts
Snow drips blood
liberty breaks out
hold a flag bloodied
of the Lieutenant's hands cut off

Anna Banasiak
POLAND

Anna is an award winning poet, literary critic and occupational therapist. Her poems have been published in New York, London, Australia, Canada, India, Africa, Japan, China and Israel. She has had many books published including *Duet of Tears* an English-Japanese poetry book co-authored with Noriko Nagaoka, *Duet of Waves*, an English-Japanese poetry book co-authored with Yoshimasa Kanou, and *Duet of Masks*, English-Persian poetry book co-authored with Afrooz Yafarinoor.

E: banama7@wp.pl

THE HARP

Jerusalem
I hear the yearning in your voice
Rashi's commentaries are hidden in the rustle of trees
The stones are full of mystical light
Music seeps in the garden of sounds
The Psalms of David echo eternity
In the shadows of the past
I find the promise
Of peace
The harp drowns out
The cry of war

LindaAnn LoSchiavo
USA

LindaAnn is a dramatist, writer, and poet. Her poetry chapbooks *Conflicted Excitement* (Red Wolf Editions, 2018), *Concupiscent Consumption* (Red Ferret Press, 2020), and *A Route Obscure and Lonely* (Wapshott Press, 2020), along with her collaborative book on prejudice (Macmillan in the USA, Aracne Editions in Italy) are her latest titles. She is a member of The Dramatists Guild and SFPA.
Blog: maewest.blogspot.com

THE WALL (WASHINGTON, D.C.)

So many years since a chopstick click of yes:
You promised you'd return. I vowed I'd wait.
Since Uncle Sam's jets didn't hesitate,
I kept attacking doubts as I caressed
Your name between thick lines of words compressed,
Hoping my fortune cookies foretold clues,
Separating fatality from you.
One more unending war peaceniks protest.

Disorienting Nam accounts make news,
Jewels LBJ can wear or finger. Hopes
Invent what truth would never have spoken.
It's Immanent Will. War's dice throw will choose
Whose name's between thinned lines. Love envelops
This wall where a silence has been broken.

Note: The Wall - The Vietnam Veterans Memorial is a 2-acre U.S. national memorial in Washington, D.C. It honours service members of the U.S. armed forces who fought in the Vietnam War, service members who died in service in Vietnam/South East Asia, and those service members who were unaccounted for during the war.

THE BOMBARDIER

My father slowly lost his vision though
He didn't see it coming. His teenage
Face, tilting upwards, studied Brooklyn's sky
On Independence Day. Bright flashes flung
Towards heaven - Roman candles, comets - spoke
In German: mortars, aerial shells, mines.
His family watched as Hitler hogged headlines:
Annihilation, concentration camps.
When Uncle Sam knocked, he surrendered thick
Italian hair, mock manhood's pompadour.
Unlike shorn Samson, he felt stronger, believed
That if G.I.s hoped, fought for victory,
The universe would pay attention, might
Mold wanting into bold reality.
His twenty-twenty was not good enough
For flight school - only adequate to gain
Eligibility to jump from planes.

The bomb squad stayed intact, forever friends,
Fired off missives, air-mailed, unafraid,
Creating camaraderie tighter
Than elbow room inside their Air Force plane.
Survival, sex, salvation strengthened them.
The baby boom rewarded bravery,
Peace spinning into gold reality.

Their pilot went blind first, his vision peeled
Away like sunburnt skin. But Uncle Sam
Disavowed all responsibility
As, one by one, they lost the gift of sight.
The universe stopped paying attention here.

My father's retinas released their grasp
Of greens and greys. He couldn't drive at night.
Newspapers' small fonts became unreadable.
Small drusen - stony granules - multiplied.
He dreamt of black-outs, Europe occupied.
He couldn't sketch the faces of fallen friends,
Lost his ability to tell claret
Apart from a Chianti Classico,
Detect a weed from grapevines, watch sunset.

Now blindness held him in captivity.

When death escorted him to quieter
Corridors, his eyes up-turned, all prepared
To face the fusillade of so much light.

Mantz Yorke
ENGLAND

Mantz is a former science teacher and researcher living in Manchester, England. His poems have appeared in a number of print magazines, anthologies and e-magazines in the UK, Ireland, Israel, Canada, the US, Australia and Hong Kong. His collection *Voyager* is published by Dempsey & Windle.
E: mantzyorke@mantzyorke.plus.com

GREEN ON BLUE

'Green on blue', they call It,
when Afghan police (or maybe
militants dressed as police)
shoot British troops. Nothing new:

yet another loved one
opens the front door,
sees a soldier on the step,
knows the worst.

Now the ritual homecoming:
the stubby grey C-17A
sinks from the blue sky
to the still, green, sunlit land,

touches down, comes to a stop,
lowers its ramp. Smartly,
soldiers bear a flag-draped
coffin to each attending hearse.

Later, young and old
stand in silence at the roadside,
unshowily, their heads bowed,
as the cortege passes by.

Green on blue – the glory
of an English summer day
once more turned upside down
by the converging lens of grief.

ZERO

We'll show 'em, we said.
No-one told us Spitfires
couldn't twist and turn like Zeros
but should fight instead
on the dive and climb.

The Zero in my sights
loops the loop, disappears
behind. Bullets slam
into my engine, fuselage,
fuel tanks and wings.

Fire! I'm screaming
down to altitude zero –
the soft-rippled, cerulean
sea whose surface I know
will be harder than stone.

WAR GAME

The terraln tllts, swerves
on his console
as he manoeuvres
the distant drone.

He enters co-ordinates
for the target, the missile locks on,
then ZAP! In a flash,
mud bricks are rubble and dust.

The second, exploding
among scrabbling villagers,
completes the mission.
Game over.

Later, evaluators
send back news:
the incorrect co-ordinates
will be excused.

Fred Krake
USA

Fred currently lives in Nebraska USA. He is now a professional mentalist. Previously had a long career in executive protection and running the doors at various bars and clubs. His poetry has previously been published in *The Horror Zine* and *Space Sports and Spider Silk* to name a few.
E: fred.kracke@gmail.com
Twitter: @bigfredman

BROKEN

The blood came like a flood.
Terrorized streets, as the bodies of the innocent pave the way to the
presidential seat.
All authority lost, a nation's freedom the only cost.
A soldiers oath was broken.
By the millions that were spoken.
Personal glory won.
Yet the sacrifice of the innocents has begun.

T THE GATE

Thunder at the gate,
we face an unknown fate.
Lightning and thunder,
a soul that's been torn asunder.
The bullets fly as young men die.
The glory is a lie, as the widows cry.
One soldier down, but he's gained his crown.

DYING

To die for a lie,
it will make the strongest widow cry.
To die for a brother,
will make the unknown crowd,
stand so proud.
Gun salute of twenty one.
This soldier died for the other one.

Mike Rollins
KAZAKHSTAN/ENGLAND

Mike was born, and has lived most of his life in Barrow in Furness, Cumbria, in the North West of England, working in the local shipyard until leaving to train as an English teacher. He has written poetry for many years and now works in Kazakhstan.
E: mikeyrollins@yahoo.com
FB: @microimagery

THE BLOODY THREAD

They drift Into the village,
dusty ghosts in the fading light.
Armed. Dangerous.
Tired. Frustrated.
Professional. Efficient.

All is secured by the time the Headman is brought to the officer
and asked the same question as always:
'Where are your young men?'

He knows; He does not know.

As the soldiers filter from the empty streets
the broken body is cradled in ancient arms.

The young boy has watched in silence from
the rocky slope, where his grandmother sent him to hide.
His dusty face, patterned now with tears, is set in a grim mask
when he takes the pistol from his grandfather's room.

Breaking a promise,
he walks away to war.

STONES

broken,
they fell to the ground and splintered into
golden stars
reflecting the cold snow and the hard stares of the new masters.

broken?

memory is the strength of a nation, so they remember all:
blood in the streets;
a coat for a child, sewn from a thin grey blanket;
black smoke that became swirling grey snowflakes: the ashes of
Judah.

it has been many years since she placed the first
stone
upon the step of the railway car, and now she adds
another.

because she remembers.

she remembers, so that we will not forget.

CONFLICT

where is the
meaning
in dark
whispers

or in the
colours that
we wear?

where is the
meaning
in the games
we play

or in the
weapons that
we bear?

where is the
meaning
in the myths
we make

or in the
hero's
death?

where is the
meaning
in a soldier's
words

that he bleeds
in his last
breath?

Malcolm Judd
ENGLAND

Malcolm has been writing poetry for around 20 years. Most of his work, although not all, has been written whilst suffering depression and mental illness.
E: maccyj22@hotmail.com

BATTLES

Battlegrounds in knee deep mud
Exploding shells nearby
A comrade hits the ground with a thud
Take care my dear friend
Goodbye

The hills taken the emplacements lost
Bridges saved for troops to cross
A line which must not be broken
Hold the enemy
No matter the cost
In distant history lost to time
Defiant we must remember them now
To lose our respect would be a crime
We must never forget
Somehow
The death created by others greed
Planting within us a hatred seed
To live in peace are we too blind to see
Until we learn we will never be
Free

Donna Zephrine
USA

Donna was born in Harlem New York and grew up in Bay Shore, Long island. She went to Brentwood High School, graduated from Columbia University School of Social Work in May 2017, and currently works for the New York State Office of Mental Health at Pilgrim Psychiatric Centre Outpatient SOCR (State Operated Community Residence). She is a combat veteran who completed two tours in Iraq. She was on active duty army stationed at Hunter Army Airfield 3rd Infantry Division as a mechanic. Since returning home, Donna enjoys sharing her experiences and storytelling through writing. Donna's stories most recently have been published in the *New York Times, The Seasons Qutub Minar Review, Bards Initiative, Radvocate, Oberon, Long Island Poetry Association* and *The Mighty*. Donna has participated in various veteran writing workshops throughout NYC. Recently Donna was featured *USA Warrior* stories, and took part in *Warrior Chorus* and *Decruit*, which encourage self-expression through looking as classical literature and performing it, while relating it to your own life with war and trauma. Currently Donna is studying for her licensing in social work. Donna is always seeking new experiences to learn, such as Toast Masters which focuses on public speaking. She is involved in World Team Sports, Wounded Warrior Project and Team Red White and Blue. In her spare time Donna plays sled hockey for the Long Island Rough Riders.
E: kauldonna@yahoo.com

A TRIP TO THE LONE SOLDIER

Israel, a land rich in war and religious history.
I set foot on the plane seeking a spiritual healing.
Heroes filled the plane beside me
This trip was for females across the US who had fought in combat.
A time for bonding, discovery, and healing.
We visited sights you could never imagine.
Israel had many wars hit their soil.
A land of battles
Bloodshed
Visited 9/11 memorial,
museums of war artefacts,
Ammunition Hill.
The most moving of them all was the Lone Soldier.
On Ammunition Hill stands the memorial of Michael Levin.
A lone soldier from America who moved to Israel.
At the young age of 18 he decided to fight for the country of his ancestors instead of his home country.
Dedicated himself to Israel
Became a hero of their land.
His citizenship or birth place did not matter,
His heart was in Israel.
He fell in Israel,
Fighting for the country he thought of as home.
His grave is filled with flowers, momentums, flags, baseball caps, notes, and medals.
You could feel the love Israel has for him at his grave
People from all over the world visited
Not forgotten
Not unrecognised for his dedication.

SEPTEMBER 11, 2001

A day that shook the world.
A planned terrorist attack.
When those planes hit our towers, they hit our sense of security.
Before this date the U.S felt secure, untouchable.
That day proved us wrong and fear struck the nation.
Security throughout the country increased.
Airports suddenly required thorough checks of bags, metal detectors, removal of shoes, belts, technology.
The rules and regulations more strenuous.
People fearing to fly, fearing a sudden attack.
It changed our training our troops. The reserve and National Guard's training was doubled.
National guard and reserves became mobilized into active duty
Washington felt like it was on lockdown.
Tightened security, less flexibility to the public.
Fear was apparent and filling the air.
Increased negative stigmas towards middle eastern people.
Fear turned to hatred and judgement.
The U.S was shaken and our sense of security has never been the same.

VETERANS OF THE VIETNAM WAR

The forgotten generation.
Faced hatred and shame in their own country.
Fought for their country, but left with no support.
Called baby killers,
Humiliation,
Isolation
Voices not heard.
Their minds filled with trauma.
From the war,
Battle fatigue,
Shellshock,
Hatred from their country.
No one aware.
No one to lean on.
No help was there.
To help with their struggles
But their struggles were not in vein
Brought awareness to PTSD
Paved the way for veterans today.
To get help
Be cared for
Shown compassion.
Yet the road to recovery continues to be long and hard.

Mary Anne Zammit
MALTA

Mary Anne is a graduate from the University of Malta in Social Work, in Probation Services, in Diplomatic Studies and has a Masters in Probation, and has also obtained a Diploma in Freelance and Feature Writing from the London School of Journalism. She is author of four novels in Maltese and two in English, and some of her literary works and poetry have been featured in international magazines and anthologies and set to music and performed during the Mdina Cathedral Art Biennale in Malta. Also, her artistic works has been exhibited in various collective exhibitions, both locally and abroad. In June 2018 Mary Anne was awarded the Artist of the Year at the International Art Exhibition, Mezzujuso, Sicily. In 2019 Mary Anne was again rewarded Emeritato Artistico al Maestro per alto messagio artistico, in the second Mezzujuso International Art Exhibition. In the same year Mary Anne was awarded the Art Prize Eccellenza in Onore a Salvatore Fiume in Comiso, Sicilia. Mary Anne s' art work has also been featured in *Art Ascent* and in *Rejoinder Journal* published by the Institute for Research on Women, and in *The Universal Sea, The Art and Innovation Movement against water Pollution*. In October 2019 Mary Anne participated in the Erotic Art Exhibition in London and in November 2019 she had a solo exhibition with the title *Women and Her Emotions* at Jasmine Nursing Home, Msida. He literary work has been featured in many publications worldwide including: *Literature Today, Volume 4, 5, and 6, International Contemporary Poetry Volume 4, Taj Mahal Review, New English Verse*, and in *Praxis on Line Magazine for Arts and Literature, Qutub Minor Review Vol. 1*, and in the *International Collections of Poetry and Prose's War Betrayal, Seasons, Empowerment, The Elements, Eros* and *Suicide*.
E: mariefrances3@gmail.com

THE FLOWERS OF WAR

Dead Flowers in Vase.
Birds singing,
signs of Summer.

If they ask me for my name.
I do not have one.
Because I am replica of a broken soldier.

My mind still in action.
Before the war I kissed the stars,
and dreamt of endless oceans.
She is opening her heart to me.
The woman with black hair and big lips.

She comes and kiss me
I wish to love her.
But cold memories divide us.
I only put dead flowers on her hair.
She keeps on coming.
I am nothing but a memory of war.
And I am closing, setting territories.
Afraid my flowers would kill her.
I go now.
She will not cry.
Or does she?

HOSTAGE

The golden sands of desert Gulf.
Sunset comes in.
And they pray to Allah.
Before the desert sands trembled by their shots.
Their bitter cold anger against the West echoes all over.

Every sunset that comes.
He contemplates his ghastly fate.

Days in the dark.
Mission turned wrong landed him here.
Veil of unknown awaits him.
What other fate for a hidden agent?
Caught now in wildfire.

Knock in the dark.
They have come.
And on that moment he will think of her last kiss.
It was his job to keep her safe.

They come closer now, just like her lips close to him.
Close gun.
But he thinks of the warmth between them.
He will not make it home.

And while she is alone she will learn that he died as a hero for his country.
Again the sunset comes with the prayer and the shots.
Like a devastated song.
In the desert of no return.

R. Bremner
USA

R. Bremner has written of incense, peppermints, and the colour of time since the 1970s. He appeared in 1979's first issue of *Passaic Review*, along with Allen Ginsberg and Rich Quatrone. *International Poetry Review, Oleander Review, Climate of Change: Sigmund Freud in Poetry, Peacock Journal, Bosphorus Review, Jerry Jazz Musician, Ekphrastic Review*, and *Paterson Literary Review* are a few of his journal and anthology appearances. Ron has won Honourable Mention in the Allen Ginsberg Award, and has published six print books, including *Hungry Words* (Alien Buddha Press), *Absurd* (Cajun Mutt Press), *Ektomorphic* (Presa Press), *Pencil Sketches* (Clare Songbirds Publications), and *Chambers* (New Feral Press), and thirteen eBooks. He lives with his beautiful sociologist wife, brilliant so, and frisky Plott Hound in Glen Ridge, New Jersey, USA.
E: rongnan3@gmail.com

MASSACRE

We came to a clearing, a village in the jungle.
teapot huts, and lots of activity.
Five buddies killed in a woe-sodden week.
Killed by mines and punji sticks, those evil -
smelling booby traps.
Those dirty gooks! VC scum!
So when we came to the village, we were juiced up
for Action. Vengeance is for suckers, but we have to show
'em we're not fools to be picked off
one by one.
The Colonel had told us "All the innocent ones will
be out by seven to the paddies."
So anyone left in the village Was VC for sure.
So we entered the village and lined them up.
Into the ditch, bitch!

Some of them pretended to be old and frail but
like the Colonel had said, they were doubtless
doing VC work, making punji sticks or bombs
so we put the old ones in the ditches too.
And the women, many women, with children
running round, pretending to be playing.
Probably teaching the children their VC tricks
And getting them to do VC work too.
Into the ditches, bitches!
And take your gook VC kids with you!
Rat-a-tat- tat, take that!
And just like that, the village is clean.

That's all over now, many years hence.
The Army, how funny, made a big stink
"Never Again!" they barked so loudly,
but never did anything to us grunts,
so they secretly must have known we
were right.

Now I'm 65 and I know I was right
Even though my wife left years ago, she
couldn't take the jeers and Bronx cheers.
And my punk son who turned against me,
God knows where that creep is now.

And I'm mostly alright 'cept in the early
mornings when I hear the women scream.
They must be saying "save my kids!"
And there they are, those ghost kids with their
questioning eyes, those eyes that burn me
cause I never never have an answer for them
till I break down and cry.

But I'm mostly alright.

JAFFNA, SRI LANKA, 2009

Dawn:
booming voices
ears on fire
trees on fire
life on fire
PLEASE,
Some little respite,
a recess from this hell
this dissonance of fear
that lasts from dawn till dawn

ON A TEARDROP ISLAND

this night screams of betrayal.
its dainty freshness pulls you into
a harrowing slide down a hole
into a field of burnt offerings.
where was he?
who was she?
how could they?
they alighted like butterflies
on the overgrown bushes
of your back
tipping off militia
that there you were
but like a slippery chameleon you
rise, changing both form and colour
to taste the bloody din
of a night without pity
and take your revenge
in the sweet dawn

Originally appeared in *Lips Magazine*, 2017.

Brian Langley
AUSTRALIA

"I live in suburban Perth, the capital of Western Australia with my wife of fifty plus years. My poetry has changed direction somewhat, now being mostly classified as Australian Bush Poetry; rhyming poetry which has near perfect metre and consistency of structure. I write across many subjects and perform (mostly from memory) regularly at retirement villages, aged care facilities, country festivals, service and social clubs etc., etc. I perform under the name The City Poet - this is due to me being a member of the Western Australian Bush Poets Association, many members of which have a rural background and write on rural subjects - most of my poetry is from the point of view of an Australian city dweller. My poems reflect my lifestyle, age and interests, mainly ageing, being Australian, the environment, travelling, fishing and contemporary living. I also delve occasionally into politics and history. I have self published several books as well as some audio CDs and a couple of e-books of historic Western Australian poetry."

E: briandot@tpg.com.au
W: www.Brianlangley.wabushpoets.asn.au

ANZAC – THE UNTOLD STORY

It started with a single shot that echoed round the world;
The Grand Duke Ferdinand lay dead, the flags of war unfurled
as Europe's old wounds opened up and spread their discontent
to nations far across the world. There's nothing could prevent
most countries from involvement in "The war to end all wars"
as two sides gathered allies, men flocked to join the cause.
The Germans then advanced on France, but they were driven back
to Flanders where they formed a line the Allies couldn't crack;
And neither could the Germans break the British and the French;
Two armies locked in stalemate, almost trench on trench.

And here in the antipodes, Australia and N.Z.,
the call from Mother England rang in every young man's head.
They left their jobs in townships, in cities and on farms
and joined the patriotic queues to come and take up arms.
To join the Empire in its quest to rout the German horde;
to break the deadlock on the Somme where neither side had scored.
The Aussie and the Kiwi lads, with patriotic zest
They knew that they could beat all odds, they knew they were the best.
They'd give that Kaiser Bill "what for", he'd soon be on the run;
"We're soldiers of the Southern Cross, we'll show him how it's done."

Now the Aussies and the Kiwis, they'd been to Pommie wars;
Crimea and in Africa, they'd fought on foreign shores
and found most British Officers, the lesser sons of Lords
were rarely men whose military skills would win awards.
And the lads quite often muttered, and they likely caused offense,
remarking that "His Lordship" was devoid of common sense.
For the soldiers of the Southern Cross came from a culture new
that paid no heed to titles, but to what a man could do.
The competent, they'd follow and his orders they'd obey,
But as for those, not "up to scratch" they'd likely turn away.

And back in the antipodes, the fleet had left the shore;
November one, from Albany they'd left Australia's door
bound for Mother England via Suez and the Med.
Near forty ships of soldiers, sailed off in line ahead.
Bound first for England's training camps, then off to fight the Hun.
They knew that in a few short months, they'd have him on the run.
But ere two thousand miles had passed across the stormy sea
than discontent, far, far away would change the destiny

of the soldiers of the Southern Cross, in battle, yet untried,
But who, in conflicts yet to come, would be a name of pride.

In training camps in England's south, that discontent occurred;
And at the time it was hush, hush; the public never heard;
And even now, in hist'ry books, no mention you will find
that soldiers in these training camps, by MPs were confined;
For orders, they'd refused to do, they said they were "on strike."
Until conditions and their food met standards they could like.
"Impossible", the Generals said, "Get back to work before
You all are charged with mutiny. For that you know the score.
But common sense – a bit – prevailed, a stand-off for a while
So lists of issues from the troops, their spokesmen could compile.

These issues that had caused the strikes, poor food, no uniforms,
no blankets to keep out the cold wet winds from winter storms;
no guns to hone the soldiers' skills, just replicas of wood.
They'd take some time to organise, but meanwhile, if they could
keep disenchanted troops in hand, the Generals', did chime,
"Things likely could be sorted out, perhaps by Christmas time;
but only," they continued, "if we keep the status quo.
We can't let wild colonials come, they'll just make matters go
from bad to worse, they must be stopped, they'll add to discontent"

And so an urgent message to the fleet was quickly sent.

It said that as the Ottomans had joined the German cause;
the forty ships of soldiers should take a little pause
and stay a while in Egypt (till the strike was sorted out);
and be a sort of buffer should the Germans think about
sending Turkish troops to take the Suez from the Poms.
"We'll let those wild colonials have a taste of Turkish bombs."
And while our soldiers bided time, their new name came to be;
a simple acronym it was, in print for all to see.
Officially 'Australia and New Zealand Army Corps,'
Or ANZAC which replaced all names that they had had before.

And still the ANZACs waited for their chance to join the fray;
to boot the Germans out of France to send them on their way.
But fate now took a different turn, for the Ottomans had closed
the Dardanelles to shipping, so the British then proposed
to send an allied naval force of warships (obsolete),
to clear the mines and stop the guns; to give the Allied fleet
access to Sevastopol, with weapons and supplies
for the Russian Cossack forces who planned for the demise
of the Germans on their Eastern Front; but all did not go well;

for the Allies were defeated and their ships were blown to hell.

And so it was decided, (as they couldn't win by sea)
on a land based assault on the guns, across Gallipoli.
And though there would be casualties, upon that Turkish coast
The Dardanelles they'd open in a month - or two, at most.
For on the ground, in Egypt, were half the needed men;
the ANZACs, restless, waiting, (four months they'd been till then)
And soldiers from Newfoundland, France, and India as well,
they all could join the British and they'd blast the Turks to Hell.
Near eighty thousand allied troops, it ought to be a breeze –
They waited for the dark of moon, light winds and calm flat seas.

And so it was, at crack of dawn, on April twenty five,
at beaches on Gallipoli the Allies did arrive.
But there was much confusion for their information, poor,
meant that it was the wrong place where the ANZACs went ashore;
and the only maps the British had were school maps from their teens
which showed some gently rolling hills, not cliffs and deep ravines
that the Turks who'd known for some time of the Allies on the way,
could, with sufficient numbers, keep the landing troops at bay.
And so the conflict started, but it all went oh so wrong;
Another bloody stalemate, that lasted eight months long.

And now, so many years on, we venerate that day
we landed there at ANZAC Cove, and somehow on the way
our Nations reached maturity, Australia and N.Z.
And with those other countries, we left behind our dead.
Sixty thousand Allies, and sixty thousand Turks
died on that barren point of land; but what it is that irks
is, that we were there 'by accident' we should have been in France,
but the British didn't want us, they wouldn't take the chance
that those "wild colonial" ANZACs might trigger mutiny
in the training camps of Salisbury Plain, and so it was to be
That we ended up in Turkey, upon that fateful shore -
And the legend that is ANZAC, lives on, forever more.

BRING OUR SOLDIERS BACK

Little Johnny's taken us to war
I'm buggered if I know what for
We had no quarrel with Iraq
Hey Johnny! - Bring our soldiers back

Peacekeeping's OK on our door
Bouganville and East Timor
And helping out our neighbours when
Disaster strikes each now and then

But when the Yanks say "Come and fight"
Remember – All's not black and white
Next time you're asked – just say "I pass."
And give up lickin' Bush's arse.

In 2006, the Australian Prime Minister, John Howard (Little Johnny) announced that Australian soldiers would be sent to Iraq to join those sent there by the United States of America's government, led by President George Bush.

GLORY

In the annals of my family
there are heroes by the score.
Their pictures hang on every wall,
and over every door.

Their deeds are cast in history
in every major war.
They've seen the worst of battle.
The tears, the mud, the gore.

Each picture shows a hero
in khaki, black or red.
They went off seeking glory.
They marched in line ahead.

They didn't stop to question
the words their leaders said.
They didn't know that glory's just
another word for dead.

END

THE POET
Summer 2020
Theme: On The Road

www.ThePoetMagazine.org

Printed in Poland
by Amazon Fulfillment
Poland Sp. z o.o., Wrocław

63211299R00122